Unique Poems in Contemporary China

横笔独诗天下

Jinyong Chen

陈进勇

Intorduction: God poet Chen Jinyong

God poet Chen Jinyong is the author of the trilogy " Joy of God," "God Poet ," "My poems and my life"

This book is a collection of three works: " UNIQUE POEMS IN CONTEMPORARY CHINA". Without the author's authorization , no unit or individual shall publish , selected , adapt, translate , copy, reproduce , reprint , spread the content of this book.

Jinyong Chen's Email address: cjy282828@163.com

If you've read his poems and thought worthy of your donation to support God poet create more good poetry. Contributions account as follows :

China Postal Savings Bank Account: Chen Jinyong

Card Number: 6217996100034077956

Chen Jinyong Alipay account : cjy282828cjy@163.com

Contents

Part I: Joy of God 15
    Calendar 16
    Poets and Poetry 17
    Snake 24
    Birthday 26
    Joy of God 29
    Requiem 31
    The poet's fate 34
    The poet can not do anything 36
    Young life should know 38
    Dogs and God 39
    Gambler 41
    Male songs 43
    The man selling oranges and the words 45
    Orphans Song 48
    Midnight cry 51
    The leaving song 54
    Misty life 55
    Window portrait 56
    A person must hold a holy soul 57

Wedding Song	58
Call from daughter	60
Watermelon Song	63
Life is a dream	64
Woman's mouth and heart	65
The living song	66
The drunken song	67
Feeling of livings	68
The tea seller and the wealth	69
Persvading my father	73
Hard to be a fahter	74
Farmers' worry	75
Kite	76
God's desire	77
New Year Message	79
Bird	81
Heart	83
The Butterfly complain	85
Salvation of souls	86
Ship with people	87
Embarrassment of watching the Street	88
Sincere heart is hard to find	89
People write poetry about people	90

Poetry for mother 91
Don't be a poet 94
To Ms Ying 96
Meet in the rain 98
Say goodbye in the nigh 99
Hard to sleep 100
Song of worry and love 101
Good to have love 102
The mid-automn night and Ying 104
The naked god 106
Poem 108
Confessions of a lady escort 109
The relatives are crying for you 110
Soul monologue 112
The wine, the happiness and the home 113
Wandering Songstress 114
Words to my husband 117
Walking on the streets 120
Living in this world 121
It's hard to be the wife of poet 122
Father's love in the heart 124
Feeling in the winter night 125
Helpless sad 126

Taste the woman 127

With my son, without love 128

I think 129

Living without the memory 130

A crying man 131

The feeling and life 133

People behave like Beer 136

Poet and pig 137

The bad boss 140

Feeling when I was sick 143

The dream and life 145

Don't be too bad to yourself 146

The miracle is caused by yourself 147

Prositutute's heart 149

Repentance of the heart 151

Pray for my dead dog 153

Cannot live like this anymore 155

The life doesn't believe tears 158

The sad tears in the dream 159

The wine for the wine ghost 160

We must bite the bullet 161

Destiny of the poet 163

There will be the last day of the evils 167

After dead	169
Don't believe the writers	172
The song for my thirties	174
Hard to find the right person	175
Quack - helpless poet	177
The small family and love	180
Sank helpless	182
Make poem	184

Part II: God Poet 186

Live, live for the clean souls	187
An ordinary heart with aimbitions	189
Be good to your life	190
Miss the dog	192
Misfortune and happiness	193
Reading in the cold night	195
Seeking the lost poet heart	196
The clean souls and the poem	198
Read Poem and do nothing	199
Lie down to see and knee down to read	200
Who is doig evil on the street	201
The nake poem heart	203
The pure poet	205
The asking from the heart	208

The forever support	211
Speak for the death	214
Our spiritual homeland	218
Easy to sell meat, hard to sell poem	220
The poet and writer	221
The gambler's fate is upon himself	222
For my wift Aying	225
Giood days	228
The lover online	230
Love in the unkown place	232
The love cannot be measured	234
The love from the poets	235
The sad evning	237
Make the love to the end	238
The heartbreaking night	240
The love at the end of the world	241
The coward's love	243
Cannot love or hate you	246
The preface before the poem march	248
The missing heart is still missing	253
The worrying heart's worry	254
The lovers' in spirit	256
The love like Coffee candy	258

The best woman	259
The hurt and love	261
The best lover in life is my wife	263
The lonely wolf	266
The flying heart with love	268
The rhythm of love	271
Talk about love	274
The four word truth	276
Without love, I would rather leave	278
The woman's heart and love	280
I am saying goodbye to you	283
Complain about husband	286
We cannot compete with time	290
The arts of football	292
The good wife does not manage husband	294
Successful businessman	296
Move away from Guangzhou	298
Please call home	302
The slave of real estate	304
The Sun in the heart	306
The car models	308
The world of dream	311
About these experts and professors	314

The poet shouldn't have a marriage and family 316

Hard to get a true female friend 319

The real meaning of life 320

Only the emotional women have the true love 323

The last stage of life 326

Readers cannot understand poets 328

To thoese city administrators in China 330

Live 334

How to get a good wife 336

To HanHan: be nice 339

The dream talk with my wife 343

Leave the dream to the reality 346

The fishing activities by the city administrators 349

Poem is getting bad and people are getting old 353

The sound from the lawyers 355

Give the good police image back to me 358

To the news reporters 360

The last paradise 365

To some advertisors 369

Stay away from the small coal miners 371

The man is not man, the sea is not sea 375

The money that you cannot understand 378

The song of the drivers 379

The words from Buddha 382

Give the peaceful world to us 386

The poet thinking about life 390

About the Maotai Wine 395

To the friendship between China and Pakistan 397

The man and the poem... 400

Waiting for Jiao Yulu coming back 402

Respect knowledge and culture 406

The man who owe the balance... 407

Poetry was contrary 409

To be a good man 410

The life-survival skill of the wealths 412

where is the poem heart 413

Bad spirit hard to endure... 415

Hate Japan, love China 416

The degree seller's university 418

Begonia poem Dream 419

The lives of Ants 421

The efforts of poets are meaningless 422

Cheer for many highway toll stations 424

The heart of the hero... 426

Shaolin Monks is a merchant... 428

The poem's authenticity 430

The aim of writing and meaning of life 433

On Poets' Ineffective Life 435

Part III: My poems and my life 438

 God is calling for the real poet... 439

 Why the first class poet cannot life happily 441

 The achievement of the bad people 443

 Poet lives worse than pig 444

 Don't marry a poet.. 448

 An interesting poet.. 450

 Everything is meaningless 452

 Life with wife and poem.. 455

 Guilin's beautiful landscape 457

 Dream of Guilin... 460

 My wife is so good 462

 Good and bad to be a worker 463

 Good to talk about virtue 467

 Poor people and the new year 469

 What does my wife look like? 471

 The good Wuliangye 473

 I would like to live in the world of poem.................................... 475

 Safe milk.. 478

 Save my last good will... 480

 Poet's debts and dreams... 483

Poet's soul and body 485

The lonely poem heart 487

Heros drive carefully 490

Poem is better than writer 492

A poet does not follow the rule 495

Poet should be punished 497

The hundreds of mertis of poet 502

Worker on the production line 504

Feeling of lottery lover 505

Guilty in front of the poets 507

The feeling of doctors' parents 509

The life reflection of poet 513

Good bye, Chinese score team 515

We must save the skillful poets 519

Life is so real 523

Life is floating and poem is forever 526

Soul back to the poem way 531

The dragon from the poor house 534

The poem to save the average life 536

The poet selling poems on the street 539

The true poet living in their own heart 542

The city is a mill machine 547

The meaning of a poet's life 549

The happy parents in the Heaven 551

Get ready for the war, friends 554

Part I: Joy of God

Calendar

The deading

Register

One page

One step

Approaching the tomb

One step

One page

Recording into the history

Poets and Poetry

I chose this path

I paid a heavy price

Three years, the full three years of repression

So my body and mind have been a big blow

Poetic in my mind churn hit

Surging would break my chest

I still repressed, repressed, repressed again

At this moment

Not casually pouring

At this moment

I also have to deal with taboos and

I can not, can not, can not arbitrarily lyrics

I can not, can not, can not express what comes naturally

How many days and nights

How many times a great poet

I have repressed, repressed, repressed again

Live in poverty

Spirit against

I have patience, patience, patience again

Hard struggle

Only I know

My real value

As long as I die

I will never fall

As long as I'm alive

I certainly want to achieve my will

I believe

I never disappoint myself

I believe too

I have the ability

I was born in poverty

I'm going to rise in poverty

I was in the Suffering

I'm going to stand in the Suffering

Although the reality is so cruel

Although there is no reason to say alive

It can be used as a true poet

The courage to fight out a very brilliant way

Let frustration become difficult to defeat the enemy under my head

I always have to keep in mind

A person should have a strong will

People should realize their ideals tenaciously

Only animals

Lower animals only rely on their own instincts life

Only animals

Low IQ was a bigot animals to live

Whatever

Groaning is not my calling

Lament not my voice

My head is a symbol

Laughing is my mettle

When I picked up a pen

I can unusual people

When I picked up a pen

I was inspired by squeezing life

I was destined to go through all sorts of torture

When I picked up a pen

I will shoulder the historic task

World of mankind

Dedicated his greatest contribution

Poetic Spirit want me to do is

Spirit is poetry to me so go

Poetic inspiration all the time calling me

FIG wealthy individuals can not go to comfort

Your hands are the inescapable burden

You have to create a better future poetry

So that people here happy joy

So that people here awakening sentiment

Material wealth

Cannot substitute for your wisdom

The lure of money

You can not replace the passionate poetry

Money wealth is only temporary, superficial and desires

Only your wits

It is eternal, inherent, noble

Everything suggests

Far less than the wealth of riches wisdom

Wisdom wealth is wealth that can not be measured by money

Yeah riches

Often by skillfully taking that makes some people thrive

Not to mention whether or not come clean and appear light

Wealth can wisdom

But it is reality does not allow false

The former can have custom

The latter have greater odds

No rush to gain foot peg teeth

For the wisdom of mining Immortal Fame

At times my heart beating

My inspiration Keke in flash

As long as I have life, as long as I live

I would never, never lay down my pen in hand

I want to send the passion of destruction

I want to call, I want to shout

I have to say, I thoroughfares

This is a kind of world

Beauty and ugliness, evil and good contest

Unceasing, again and again entangled Crue

Movies out how many pieces of Heroically sad sight

However, history is always forward

Unlimited Social Development

Then a high price must be paid for the new era

Everything becomes a reality

Sad sad, praise praise

Time will heal wounds

Note left forgotten in the memory

He disappeared before the generous regret

I love my poetry than love of my life

I love my life I must love poems

Poetry aroused my survival instinct

Poetry inspired me more than struggle

Console the people give me poetry

Poetry gives me strength

Poetry, my life partner

Poetry, my life is the gene

Poetry, and poetry is my only friend togetherness

Poetry, poetry is the only friend I have one mind

I love poems

Because poetry distinguish good and bad

I love poems

Because poetry has a sense of justice

I love poems

Because I live poetry Guidelines

I love poems

Because poetry taught me Zuoren

I love poems

Because poetry lives in cottage hierarchy

I love poems

Because poetry gathered the essence of human wisdom

Poetry, poetry only make me happy joy

Poetry, poetry only make me rejoice

For myself, for the motherland and humanity

Work in the world of poetry

Because poetry

Having unteachable, can not learn the meaning

Because poetry

Require innate talent inspiration

I do not give up poetry

May 30, 1990

Snake

Do not be afraid my soft body

The winding dance

As long as you are not hostile to me

I'll treat you as a lover

Dance in front of you

Teach your true purpose in life

I look at the twists and turns of the road

Forever endless forward

As long as the enemy dares to infringe

I summon the strength to lift the high head

Facing the enemy

Red tongue sticking out oath

Dead head is not in contact

I like the soft embrace of a lover girl

Silent

I just like the waving of the powerful Gangbian

Will not give up

On people of good will

I will meekly snuggle with my soft waist

Like ivy wrapped around the tree as

V with tenderness and desire

Total climbing beautiful sky

The pursuit of spiritual spring

        March 30, 1991

Birthday

When you whining

Born on earth

Your life

Today is the luckiest one

Because today

You have a chance

To come to this world

Regardless of this world

Are Beautiful or not

You can not forget today

If not today

You did not involve dead

If not today

You missed the taste of the world to taste

If not today

You hopeless human taste test Tastes

If not today

You failed to appreciate the world of laughter Nuhen

If not today

You do not know the truth of things good and evil

If not today

You do not know the world of good and evil, beauty and ugliness

If not today

This world without you

With today because

Have your life

If you want to thank God

You gave birth to the world of opportunities

You have to first of all thank the parents

You created a complete

God gave you

Just a moment of luck

Let you have a birthday today

Parents gave you

It is the essence of the whole organism

So you have to fight the capital

God gave you opportunities

Parents have given you life

If you really want to have a better future

If you really want to create a colorful world

Today you have to remember

Birthday is your starting point

Your life is turning today

        April 7, 1991 for my own birthday

Joy of God

As a poet I

Before I did not get royalties

I had to live an ascetic life

Vegetarian is my duty

Eating meat is my sin

Impoverished me

Having something to eat is just great

Without regard to secular eyes

Belly wrapped in cloth of modesty

Ragged this does not matter

What makes me most uncomfortable is

Hungry to read

Anti-earned spiritual

We can not overcome the will of hungry

God's advice

I had no choice in the "hunger strike"

I have been wandering in the streets

Suffered through midnight flavor

Once the train counterparts

Step back to my distant homeland

We had a night raid in the mountains and remote places

Persecution by the villain villain

There have been four people begging for help

All suffered supercilious cold shoulder

Step by step toward despair are

They had suspected their ideals

My life incompetent

He had to endure the pain of the world

Ideological Benz

Burst soul

Not the original body of the opponent

I am a self imbecile

In any social era

All must be the world's most desperate torment

Students say to me

Worse than dying

Death is the most joy of God

      November 21, 1991 and in hunger

Requiem

Night has come

rest in peace

The world will people died

God will forgive your mistakes during his lifetime

Born descendants will remember your kindness when

rest in peace

Weizheng your eyes closed

Open your lips closed

All your anxiety

People will have to bear

rest in peace

Your mission has been completed

Your contribution to the world has already accepted

Remaining

Let young men to do

The bell has sounded

rest in peace

The world will be the salvation of souls

God's messenger has been calling you on the road

Heaven has lined Souls

rest in peace

Put your hands hang down exalt

Put your feet straight buckling

All labor

People will have to bear

rest in peace

Your task has been completed

Your achievements the world has long been recognized

Remaining

Let future generations to create

The song has been played

rest in peace

The world will want to leave the ghosts

God has for you gracefully festivity

You're just the gods of heaven on a

rest in peace

Trapped under your chest to straighten

Rickets settle your waist

All hi-hing

We will have to congratulate the gods

rest in peace

Your future has been to heaven

You no longer the world stage

Stay

Let the world come to dominate

	December 3, 1991

The poet's fate

As a poet

It should be understood

Things are not given good wishes

Life just gives you a sad way to go

Then a brilliant career

It can only be built on the suffering of the world

Poet sacred duty entrusted by history

Students did not give joy when

Life needs poet singing

But did not return to happiness points

Ordain

They are subject to all sorts of challenges

Maybe

The poet was born more sensitive than others

The world and it was more painful to feel easier

This has resulted in

The poet's fate

It is a painful and sad fate

Of the world grievance discontent

But fate also cannot eliminate all the challenges for human

That is the root causes of all the sadness

                                December 6, 1992

The poet can not do anything

As a poet

It is difficult to control yourself

And understand real-life

Sailing voyage

It is alone lone sail boat

Wind and waves are in the siege all the time

They just want to kill you quickly

With the sweeping shake

Yeah appeal

Only their voices heard

It is the real voyager

Nor for your troubles grief

only you

Recognize their beacon

Beautiful flawless Cantos

The anchorage

Is Poet Wei-ling

Difficult life

So that the poet can not fit

Interpersonal painful

The poet daunting

In this desperate day

How can we forget the sad life of anguish

Only this ideal world of poetry

He was entrusted with the poet infinite desire

                                        December 20, 1992

Young life should know

Young Life

You should know

You should love the world.

Not physical possessing it

The beautiful life

Is not just sexual pleasure

Please tear off those masks

Money is the demon

In the money dominate

Revealing the naked face of mercenary

And that people can not see the flesh creep

Flowers might open in the pernicious influence

Nobu reputation but not in the ugly

Love is not affectionate on the surface

Love is the soul of each other in common

Love can be born under a false authority and swords

Love is the world that can not dominate itself.

February 6, 1993

Dogs and God

Dogs and God

Oh Jinyong Chen

You are my God

Is my master

I am your dog

He is your most loyal friend

Oh Jinyong Chen

My venerable God

The world's most beloved master

Please do not cry sad

But this world is nothing more human face

Goucai loyal only to you

Your dearest she would go by her

Going to rain, the mother will marry from

This is a helpless thing

Only your poor daughter

My little master motherless year and a half

Oh Jinyong Chen

My venerable God

The world's most beloved master

Please do not cry sad

Your dearest she

You can only share happiness

We must not spend your hard

Only Goucai took the main lean

Your dearest she would go by her

Water flows downwards with the flow

This is a helpless thing

Only the poor in the future you and I, she

We must depend on each other

                                                June 27, 1993

Gambler

Dark corner

A group of people who bet on dog eat dog

Holding, sitting, standing

Gold eyes fire eyes to see cards

Figuring how to win opponents put cards

Hands trembling

Good heart in ecstasy dealer

Bad cards by heart pumping cool

Winners always want to get rich

The loser always wanted to be salvaged

Win when

Always feel the money is so easy to come

It was relaxed and happy with flowers

Lose time

Always feel regret gamble

It is so difficult to find despair

Smoke burning

Blood-red eyes relative

They regard the fate of betting on cards

It is not just the fate of the gambler

> August 8, 1993

Male songs

Please bring your head back up

All man in the world

Singer of life is not weak weak coward

Cheerful music is not powerless moan

Please give your ignorance alarm sounded

All the world's conscience baby

Happy life is not its debauchery empty talk

Erotic pleasure is not a noble sentiment brutality

Depletion of the agenda for what love

Even beauty can not be like a lover for her desperate

please remember

As a man

Dimension should not only live about a woman

God was a woman can tolerate vulgar

God did not tolerate was the man of inaction

A bloody MAN

It should be born upright

In business

The rationale is unique, dominate the party

September 22, 1993

The man selling oranges and the words

Selling oranges

Young and old things just to fill its belly

When the gutter poet becomes a fruit vendor

Bitter things

Aspirations blighted dreams are difficult

Awkward arguing on weights

Discuss price made things boring

Graceful girl comes with slim body

Do not say anything, do not indicate

Do not ask the price to pick oranges

Yellow big heart filled

I can never sell

What reason is not selling oranges

Just tell them that I cannot accept dirty money

Anger from the heart, the evil side of the gall bladder from birth

Pointing fingers on my nose and shouting

All men are the same

Do not fake Jun lofty words

Let us now say

There are official sleek

Promising's treacherous

Promising work snobbery

Promising farmers ignorance

Corrupt officials, corrupt rotten fortune

Waste of resources, damage the country

Eat and drink, including the flesh and blood

This is dirty money! This is the stench of credits

Saying when I was a young woman

Girl of eighteen, eighteen-year-old dream

Youth eighteen, eighteen-year-old Love

Music is not for people to forced prostitution

Not only immoral whore whore

There are clients and Bustard Head

Ruined humanity do not just sell smile woman

Well dressed brute hypocrite

The hacked in pieces is not true massagers

But those pious wolf dressed in human skin

But for those forced to pull people into the water trick pimp

To tell the truth

Aunt of how can I be degrading to the point

You stink even sell fruit despise

Alas! Lost your family's face

September 25, 1993

Orphans Song

Children

Please listen to meditation

Orphans of God now to tell you built

You must unite

Unfortunately, the world of children without parents

The law of the jungle in the real world

You must have a maintenance entity of interest

Desperate cries and tears cheap

We can not exchange the truth a bit! Few zealous

Even your own parents

Also like to abandon you

Ruthless world, chilling dead

Only you can save yourself

All unfortunate orphans

You must establish a strong belief

And indomitable ambition

please remember

Orphans of God's creed

Poor can Jian

Rich may moderation

No father and mother can help children

More is to create performance-based sources

By their parents, rely on others to get rich

It is sterile and children

Against powers, against shady practices

It is left smelly shameless hypocrite villain

Only on their own, relying honorable mind

I was proud glory

The world can not enjoy father, mother love children

You need to understand the world of gratitude,

And the ability to distinguish right from wrong

Please understand that

Your parents adults

Although the dead can not be held

Surviving minor children abandoned

All difficulties and excuses

We can not deprive the child's income

Regardless of any selfish behavior of young children

Parents are losing the stigma of duty

We can not wash away the sins of love buried

Parents do not love their children

Respect of always be condemned conscience

November 10, 1993

Midnight cry

Daughter

My dearest in the world

It is the morning of January 5, 1994

In your sleeping time

But I do not know your father tears his face

I really want to tell you

My lovely daughter ah

But you only two years old, two years old oh

You know what

You will not know to stop Lianku

How can you get experience this moment of father

Daughter

I'm not afraid to say to you

Now we can through thick and thin and only white dog

Dogs in trouble and did not leave us

And your mother was really abandon you

Can you ignorant

Only to know that you want to play to eat daddy crying

Do not understand the suffering of being heavy fall on his head

Oh salsa, salsa

My dear and beloved daughter

Maybe someday

Would you say dad's bad for you

But I do not know my father with tears you with big

For you

There is only a good father

Ah daughter, her daughter

I'm stroking your innocent sleeping face

But I hope you are now adults

Can you share the pain of father

Love your mother is your father's talent

Decidedly not difficult with comorbid with us

We did leave because my father was too poor

Her happiness you will not be built in my body

You woke up

Salsa, my dearest daughter

Please forgive your father you wake up to fight the tears

Dad compassion difficult to stop, tell the hard stop

You go to sleep, the night was dark

Stop this weeping to a good sleep

I love you - salsa

Only my father would really pain you

January 5, 1994 in the morning

The leaving song

Thunder is on

Rain is falling

Ghost is weeping in the middle of the night

Mr Chen had plenty of courage to be a man

But who knows him?

Do not cry for the children love their homeland

Here is not a place to succeed

Better to go to a foreign land

Least you can be a better person

Therefore, the life of hero is usually short

If you don't believe it,

Check the profile of Zhang Yimou

His brilliant life comes from poor experience

March 30, 1994

Misty life

Always life is so hard

Man had to be a man

Prefer not to say words against their conscience

Do not want to do wicked things

But the invisible hand can push comes to you

Human norms and cultural training

Corruption in the stink of money

Social drink spicy wine

Innocent dreams of youth and high school in

Lost on helpless

What are people living for in the end

The Prophets may even do not know

April 12, 1994

Window portrait

A long time can not forget

Is that you pretty shadows

That wonderful icon

Whenever you appear in the window

My heart will arouse infinite emotion

I do not know what to describe you go

You say you are Castle

Thou it green

You're talking about Green Lake

It is more than you heartbreaker

If you are angel

But you are so practical reality

Born on earth

That you are a goddess

You can be more amiable than her

Fascinated me

what are you

You are my heart in the wonderful image

April 15, 1994 in North Yulin

A person must hold a holy soul

Please hold

Purity of our conscience

Despite the dirty world

keeping it

Good people suffer

Bad guys enjoy life

Intestinal fat brain full round amusement beauty

Marry a dog's genius ugly live

But our inner world

The total for the wonderful clean

Social realities

Although we can not dominate

Holy soul but does not allow us blurred

Others can be boring to live life like a beast

We must not become lust, blinded

Because: We are the people who came to this world

Not distort the conscience of animals

                                April 23, 1994

Wedding Song

Toast

Our beloved friends and relatives

And distinguished guests, Heke

Drinking cup delicious wedding

Please bless our beautiful wedding

Please sing song for our combined German

In this moment of bliss

We sincerely hope that we indulge in the joy

Please offer flowers and wine for our bride

Praise her beauty, virtuous, sweet

Please for my wife to offer her cloth and sewing

Early congratulate her children a good hard-working

My dear bride

Please call our musicians

Our wedding song played on a

Because

Our sweet life has begun

Because

We have formed a happy family

Better human life awaits us

Lucky Star God waving to us

Ask our Almighty God bless

Our marriage happy

We live in a beautiful life

Bring it on

My lovely wife, beautiful

Faithful companion of life's journey

Let us hand in hand

To pay tribute to our men and women visitors

Thank them

The sincere wishes

Good wishes

Let us work together

Tomorrow the world

May 1, 1994

Call from daughter

Father ah father

My distant father

You know your daughter in your calling

Calling me the only respectable amiable person

You're gone, you're gone

I can not cry sad to leave your

I only get desperate cry

You step back to see the

I know that you have to go

Our dogs tell me

Our host for our life on the run

Father ah father

My distant father

Although your daughter is only two years old and more

The kindergarten has not taught me to write

But, I have blue eyes wrote "nostalgia"

Every time I tearful farewell

I hold your legs, I bite your clothes

You are determined to leave

We just take care of the dog choked

Father ah father

My distant father

I am most pleased that your return

That no one dares to bully me

I want to eat, I want to play by You

I want to hold, that you are happy to be back

I am most happy is riding on your shoulders

Chase our dog

Father ah father

My distant father

It puzzled me the most is the kindergarten

Why teach us to sing the old world only a good mother

Mom looks like I do not know what long

There is only a good father is really

Dad did not have to hold children

Father ah father

My distant father

When is your return date

I am waiting with my dog in the village.

But I cannot see you.

May 15, 1994

Watermelon Song

Ugh

Exhale to the sky

Day does not help as my willing

Tired of watching the clouds come rolling

Watermelon is round

It praises intentionally

When launching ruthless

People say watermelon is sweet and delicious

People know what's good stuff is not the case

Talented have to sell watermelons

This is a good man washing face

Watermelon bitterly mind song

When can improve the plight

A painted melons is my courage and loyalty

        Selling watermelons May 27, 1994 in Yulin Street

Life is a dream

Midnight quiet man

Tears flooded the pillow

Dark sky

A few high stars

Embellishment is desolate boundless

Life is short

Just like a meteor

Youth is so volatile

Faint moonlight spend Ends

Silent Silent

As the water half

That night too

                                                June 2, 1994

Woman's mouth and heart

Please do not believe the woman's mouth

Today, given that they love you

Tomorrow he will be able to talk about love

In fact, a woman's heart is floating grass

Always follow the crowd

If you really listen to the woman's mouth

It must be difficult after the same comorbidity

More women murmuring

Promises

It is more likely to cheat you

Love broken heart and liver

If you really believe that a woman's heart

That must be the performance after the storm

Wishing intentions were more women

This heart often have different

You should be more mentally prepared

Take to heart the point

                                              June 10, 1994

The living song

The world is heartless

Renyi light as wool

Do not rely on relatives and good friends

There are all selfish

World is Bitter

Suffer in silence own comfort

Do not expect others to understand your worry

Living up to snobbery

No one will work with you when you have no money

Things is difficult

Life comes through temple

Complex of suffering by myself

Do not forget the past

A man can only sing the song today

July 21, 1994

The drunken song

Live in the money-oriented word

Get drunk

Fishy light sweat whom contention

Ye poverty

Or Wealth worth mentioning

Fame is just too ephemeral

Ugh

Climb to the top for several times

Life is short

Laugh bitterly

Sing a song when cry

Die from doing nothing

Is even not as good as being an antique in today's world

July 25, 1994

Feeling of livings

Life

So that they are helpless alive

Ordinary beings

Struggling in the intrigues

LIfe

Is really boring

Dead

Is also not substantive significance

Reproduction of human remains

August 2, 1994

The tea seller and the wealth

Selling tea served tea in the shade of the South

August heat wave climate forcing

Leisurely galloping black crown

Chating stop riding the next step

Developed by holding fishing rod

Your old man whispered tea

Is there a good drinks

The man whispered slowly

I only sell Nanshan old tea

Cup of tea, then you'll feel the power

White eyebrows

Who can be described as healthy longevity

Nothing else to sell tea Fun

But away from the Red lofty people

Good nose face true gentleman

Life do not do good conscience

Ugh

You also make tea talkative

Do not blame the old lady straight mouth words

Seventy seventy years of age is not lived

Life inaction will be an idiot

My wife is selling tea

Life is not what I can tell you

This is the day to face the

Evil mind outside unclear

Gentleman is the word play

Generation of reactive power on a guilty conscience

Saying I then wanted to join the army

Wife turns out a crying two three hanging bar

Life and death would not let me join the army

I had no choice but to university

And then the war horses swirling chaos

Reading scholar also suffer

Science is not a line of business

Since ancient times, they made light parting businessman

Light wife forgot a year for two years

Three abandoned wife married concubines

Four years left embrace the right to hold love mistress

Five were thrown from the ancestors to live in song

Ugh

Everything had wasted years

Powerless regret wife

Oh

Old man old people-strong

The children of this crime Bese

Two prayer Road to Life things

Interest-free for the world's workers

Since the start in order to thrive

The bitter struggle to succeed

Wealth worth coming off the ground

I abandoned young workers travel channel

View firms seen and heard

Antiaris knife to profit

Trading is not a small child drama

Every word is under sentence to earn money

They do not recognize their relative

Sending more money is most amiable

After the party developed consciousness

Life sincerely seek hardest

How many rich ugly face

Last part really is not worth a child

Ugh

People ah people

However the word value Comments

Is sincere or bad

August 25, 1994

Persvading my father

This evening

Yesterday evening

Joyous dismal various

Former music

Scenic tour to join the family

Today worry

The successfulman abandoned the old woman

Wine comes

Night song comes

The new did not see the old one cry

I hate the old man

Forget old friends

And do not come home in the night

The Tears in the children's faces

Worry about thehome

Do not want to harm the young spirit

        September 16, 1994

Hard to be a fahter

Quiet village

Thick darkness

Innocent daughter sudden get ill

Urgent! Urgent! Urgent

Acted as a father and a mother

Hard! Hard! Hard

The evening of 1 October 1994

Farmers' worry

The gold, yellow wheat

Everyone in the world are required to eat

Three meals a day, night night

Jun mouth belly who sense

The children, and the green field in the world

Can I ask how many bitter the life is

Even the ten thousand ares green wave cannot obscure worry

October 5, 1994

Kite

Do not let me calm down

Silence is not my temperament

If you really love me

Please pull your love string

Let my love flying in the sky

You might be angry with me

But you have to work with me

I can withstand your storm

But I can not afford the fact that you give up in silence

Please hold the line between us

I follow it how much risk there is

October 1994 30 nights

God's desire

Please remember

God gave us the head to think

Not want us to become the generation that came with moderation

Lord gives us thinking

In order to expect us to be assertive

Thinking, study the root causes of things

Sincerely pray for God's people

Not always understand God's desire

God do not believe will be a miracle pray

Development of things

God Almighty really do not know

Establishment of the soul dominate, notion of

Ecstasy is no master at play

please remember

God gave us hands

We should not hold the idle mind is called "Amen"

Lord gives us strength

In order to transform the world expect us to

Make a difference, to create a new world

Sincerely beg God's people

In fact, we do not understand God's wish

God do not believe will be given to beg

Worldly things

Amen can not grasp

Xinchengzeling, I do not know the Lord

White kneeling sing only for self-consolation

please remember

God gave us the chest

We have no way not to chest

Lord gives us the mind

As is the hope that we hold the sad gratifying things

Patience tough, strong faith

King Huai sincere man of God

We do not necessarily know God's intentions

King did not believe God has conceived benefits

Fireworks Room

Vegetarian also does not fully understand

No distractions, do not want to do

Restraint is skin deep

December 1, 1994

New Year Message

It's the New Year

You're not at the beginning but a continuation of Love

Over the past 365 days is to eliminate your consumption

I love you , but one day is better than one day

How many nights are full of dreams for your fantasy

Your faces and voices , your smiling face makes me yearn deeply

Love your day is really not comfortable

I was unable to resist the temptation to you my

What should I do

I admire people who have long curtain

Only you can resolve my suffering knot

Salute and Ming

Love your heart is like fireworks bloom as beautiful to you

On this festive night

Are you aware of the distance someone is to congratulate you bless

When you and your family spend Lantern Night

May you happier than me and happiness

Worth singing is our shared past

Happy days that stay forever

Now let me food for thought

I hope you and I can always return to the good times altogether

You may also have to desire

We have a new harvest in the new year

January 30, 1995

Bird

A beautiful bird flew into my field of vision

Her flirtatious soft body

My loneliness long mind affects

Fengyun restless heart beating again in the country

I can not tell you I love you

So maybe I will look bold

After all, I had been lovelorn

I do not want you to have infringed

I only put me on your long-awaited heart buried

I admit that you brought me joy and sunshine

I hope to see the field is so broad and beautiful

I struggle in the history of the passionate pride

I also admit that you brought me comfort and strength

I have support at a difficult setback, renewed

Although, I can not boast that you are the best woman in the world

You may be water, my heart is holy in Green Lake

You let me in your fish Ge children multifarious tenderness in Shiba

If you do not set off

I can not have so cute

Without your beautiful

I can not be feeling the inspiration

I hope you and me forever

Join hands in creating a better future

I would also like you not say how much I love you

You flush

March 5, 1995

Heart

When I read you

It is a kind of beauty to enjoy

Thinking of you

It is a helpless nostalgia for you

I know

You have your wish

I just want to wish you full portrait

I want to say you like it

I love you no matter whether road

Indeed you by my side

It brought me joy and happiness

Many depressing things

In your smile in resolving

In talking to you like a happy dream raving

I want to confess to you

I love how you are

I'm afraid I can watch you wrong situation

I had a little slick

Pretend like you care about big brother

Yet you also ever know how much I was embarrassed

Pretended brother is really too uncomfortable

I thought that you be my Valentine

You do not blame me

I think sweetheart

You have your powers refused to love

I forbid you do not have the privilege of Acacia

March 12, 1995

The Butterfly complain

I love you

I can not say anything

I love you

I just want to dance in front of you

Oh, the world's lover

I love you

I really want to cry for you

Why just speechless

I still fall back on you

In order to accompany you through our good times

I dance in front of you show attitude

You know I have thousands of style

Why do you ignore my presence

Oh, the world's lover

There are a few of the flowers

You'd be putting style

You will Gaogaodidi

Another doubled always feeling among

June 7, 1995

Salvation of souls

I saved my soul

But I do not fumble it where

Only feel noisy sound coax called Giant

I'm looking , I'm looking for my first arrived in the world of colors

I wash , I have spent twenty years washed atrium

I hear the nightingale calling

I saw a crow devouring nightingale meat

July 3, 1995

Ship with people

I want to escape from the turn of the wheel

It makes me too tired to live

Force me to go I want to go the way

I want to stop and take a break from step

How people want to live

I found the "people" can not single-mindedness

People come halfway

Ship pushed on different

Inconsistent with the desire

August 5, 1995

Embarrassment of watching the Street

I saw the money running on the street

I saw the shrewd businessman to put money into the store welcome

I see honest people just open shop

I also saw more people money to ingratiate

I wanted to laugh but I laugh

I cry ... I want to cry with laughter

August 20, 1995

Sincere heart is hard to find

The modern people put their sheart out

Then glorify it

Then put it in a place where we can not imagine

People write poetry about people

People write poetry, about people

We live in musical poems

We will fill the music spectrum of life

We put the bitterness of life carved into bad song

We sang, we cry, we laugh

When we cry no to elderly

When we laugh youth fantasy

When we say that children childlike

Not worth half a cup of tea in front of the old uncle

March 10, 1996

Poetry for mother

I do not know how to say hello

I can only say that you really are my mother

But, the mother does not necessarily tantamount to mom

"Mom" was what might matter to you

May be for me, "Mom" This title is too precious

You can live without me

I can leave when I chirp learn language

I can not accuse you what

However, it was in when I do not know the personnel

Now, I say to you, I appreciate you indictment

Mother, although I do not have standing in court sue you

I deserve to recover Motherhood

However, I now accuse you to sue your soul

You really owe me too

No matter how you and dad before

But, from the day that you gave birth to me

You should give me deserve something

Because: I am your daughter

Because: I am your flesh fell off! Living creatures

You have no reason, no excuse to refuse to give motherly love

You can leave dad

You can also leave me

But, you have to give me care, give me love

With maternal age children can get

You talk about whether I should get

You say there's anything I can not get

You say that you have the right to deprive what I deserve mothering

You can not give me to eat

You can not give me to wear

You can not give me live again

But, you have to give me to see you

Give me love, give me care

I have to give the world's most precious motherly love

You can not call me "daughter"

But, you do not let me call you "Mom"

Even if you let me call, I also how sad scream

Screamed so uncomfortable

"Mom," this world is not unfair

But "Mom" unfair

"Mom," and now her daughter to teach you

And it is competent to advise you

Man is not alive to the selfishness

Life is for the love alive

Their children are selfish people, selfish world it will

Their children do not care for people

People can not only for myself

Fraternity will make people live more joy and happiness

        July 22, 1996 on behalf of my daughter

Don't be a poet

World, ancient and modern

Whether a famous poet or author unknown

Able to live by its very few poems remuneration

Not to mention the poet was persecuted to death

Even if there are a few lucky poet

Although the need to wash the soul of a poet

Spirit is asking poet unpaid

Today's media culture

Perhaps poetry is no longer suitable for public appetite

The hardest thing in the world between the teachings of the soul

The most embarrassing thing is counterproductive

How can talented

Anti earn? Scream

How can numb the soul opponent

Perhaps the poet should withdraw today's literary scene

Gone are the days past scenery

Really, read poetry read out in good faith! Read a noble

Reading fiction read but pleasure! Read narcissistic

Poet in spirit and in life is ascetic

If you can not please the poet's social elite favor

Or the preferences of the rich

As a result, only one - impoverished

November 1996 26 Night

To Ms Ying

I would like and would like to say to you

Ingrid, maybe you do not care about me

I really love you

I admit that I really trivial

I will use the mortal heart - love you

I do not care after the storms of life

I will be as bad for your heart

love you love you

I told you how it is possible to export

I would like, would like to use my heart to tell you

How can you, how to be able to hear it from me

I expect people child - Liu Qingying

I hope you understand

I love you, I do not care what you have

Because: I love you I

As long as you are good to me I will grant

Big difficult for me you wore

I want to, want to touch your hands

Make you feel my blood is so hot

My heart is how surging

My feelings for you are about

My soul for you dominated

Ying ah, Ying

People who love you understand how can you tell

Perhaps one day there are so

You leave me, leave loved ones

Feel I can not let you have what

Leave me, perhaps your wisest choice

If this naive coming

I will pray for you

I hope you have a better tomorrow

Although my heartache, my tears

I can only look at you back away blessing

Beloved English better than me

I pray to God with tears

Ying always good

People who love you can not see where you worried about you

April 28, 1997

Meet in the rain

In our agreed time I come

Although the day was heavy rain

You can order - Ying, I come

I waited in the rain of you

You can not come

Unfamiliar face appeared and disappeared in the rain

Leaving the water disappointed me

I hope time will remain at the moment we meet

But time is ticking passage

I hope you can come, Ingrid - I am disappointed

Come not you, someone else

I do not recognize the face, is indescribably sad rain

I came to you Ying

Although I was hopelessly waiting for you

I love your heart is still looking forward to the rain

Pouring rain hit me immortal love you Firelight

Burning is not only my attachment to you

Ying

      May 1997 for 9 nights in Yong'an Beiliu

Say goodbye in the nigh

Motor ring

Away not just about Ying also nostalgia

Moto running

There are not just passing wilderness parting mileage countdown

Escort you are not hard - it is in terms of motorcycle

Tough my heart - and you can not say goodbye to upload suffering

Ye love you, love you no matter whether Ying

Off the star, also bid farewell to the moon

In return is owned by a single solitary backhaul

Only frogs a helpless laugh Yelang

                                        June 1997

Hard to sleep

Ask the world

Road to make the world who scores

Know you are wrong, you are wrong from

How do I treat you my darling

I had flat folk husband man

Think you are not a net result of seven

Buddhist monk can not repair the road

Do you suffer for my original

Life really helpless dead

Love is a lengthy, lengthy also hate

Who knows I love bitter thoughts

Net vulgar husband can not think your heart

May lament

Distressed lovers dream world

Yang Hsiu sound and smell tasteless

July 28, 1997

Song of worry and love

Living world has an end

Love has no regrets

Call you, Ying

Bit of helplessness bit of love

My mind is empty

Only worrying about that you are leaving me

Mismatches in person

Who says there are thousands of facts of love

Ask the people in my heart.

Do you really know?

August 30, 1997

Good to have love

I did not expect that I will recognize you

In my previous drawing

I did not give you leave position

Maybe God is Spirit disorder

We arranged acquaintance

I no longer calm calm heart Fengyun

I really can not resist the temptation to you my

What can I do? Cute Ying

Although I grovel at your feet ordinary

I can also have plain love you a heart

I often wonder

How to capture your heart

Perhaps my taste test makes me sad adventure

Everybody was afraid of experiencing the pain of failure

If I can not seize fate

I will regret for life

Such a good girl like you who will regret

God will let you drift away laughing I was a fool

The world is only fools dare chase his beloved woman

Ying let you slip away unless I do not

As long as I beat a man's heart

I'll never forget you

You will also have full strive

Hey, Ying

Love, nice

Although concerned about unhappy people but also sweet

September 1997

The mid-automn night and Ying

Several times tribulation

Twenty-known after a few cold spring and warm

Vicissitudes of life

Why do people suffer hardships contention

Ying calls out

Too many cases cross-flow filled with emotion

One thousand rustic endure fear the people to make things difficult

Bony man does not fall but their heart is fragile

Why did I have emotions heart love English

It is also willing to bitter, tired and willing

You can not help but nostalgia

Ying cry

I miss you

But also desperation, hard into the mind

Who knows my heart

Ask the heavens earth

What day reunion

A dream come true

Care to send infatuation moon

Difficult, difficult, difficult day I would like to help

                                        1997 Mid-Autumn Festival night

The naked god

Fools, do not believe in God

You better have a difficult time just believe in yourself

Everything in this world is for trading

If you are not here when the equivalent

Do not want someone to help you

Perhaps the only really help you yourself

Believe it

We are able to escape the selfish

As we able to escape death

please remember

Do not see the world so beautiful

Do not also see the world so bad

Because

Whatever our own strength too small

We can not fight and Social

We can only adapt to social development

Otherwise, only perish

Concerned about their lot, a lot of care for their own

This is really more than their own wish to care for others

Remember: God does not appear that you have a difficult time

Because: God like you trouble

October 20, 1997

Poem

Poetry

Like high white clouds drift

Although the United States can not enjoy

Poetry

Like the poor do dream of getting rich

Although misty dream but hopeless

Poetry

Like an alcoholic home reeling drunk at midnight

Let people do literary dream delirious

Poetry

We have lost the previous scenery

Poetry

It can only be left to the individual soul from the tour

Poetry

No longer as attractive as a clean new currency

Poetry

It has become a literary liar props

Like a monkey-like man playing

February 24, 1998 night

Confessions of a lady escort

Pretty woman

It is not necessarily a good woman

Perhaps behind a beautiful trap

If the temptation to let you be tempted

Greed is your instinct

Crack the eggs will not blame bites

I think you are fake, fake love you too

Accompany you just want to coax your money

Women are really flesh is true

Heart is fake, fake emotion

March 2000

The relatives are crying for you

Numerous night

You did not come back

How many days

Your home without trace

Your laughter

Your back

Your faces and voices

We have been away from

You greetings

Your care

Your Face

Have seemed so strange and hypocritical

In this there is no affection, no love at home

did you know

Your loved ones bless you

Your loved ones pray for you

Bless you for a better life

Wishing you a successful career

Pray you happy socializing

Pray you OK full

                                        May 8, 2000

Soul monologue

My heart is no longer open to people

My soul had self monologue

The troubles of life I am a man bear

Days of suffering I feel good

The mask too many people

Unable to find beautiful holy

Real life too much frustration

Looking vision is not realistic

Lonely soul wandering

Living organism in hard labor

Spiritual sustenance is hopeless pursuit

2000 May 19 Night

The wine, the happiness and the home

Ugh

Sigh

Red things

Feeling very much

For a refreshing and delicious Li River Brewery

Why come between love was

Riches and honor like a cup of beer bubbles

That is a bunch of scattered

Advise annoying things aside worldly

Frozen drink a cold beer frozen Liquan

Hug the wife funny good woman

Fun

Happiness in life

Than this

Cup of wine

Behind him through thick and thin small home

July 4, 2000

Wandering Songstress

Singing a song for the guests

I do not know but beautiful singing

How much grief and sorrow buried

We smiley usher guests

We bid farewell to the smiling faces of guests

But I do not know smiley face next

How much frustration and humiliation that says

We sang, we laughed

We sang songs in the world can narcissism

We laughed all the world's unrequited love ass

Showgirl with customers there really any emotion

But every man in each of the roles Bale

We cried

That only you can hear crying

We call

Inner voice that only you can understand

I experienced a lot of emotional pain

Numbness is love

Shen is the spirit of waste

We no longer fantasy

Hope reappears

Miracle of Love

It does not occur in our body Showgirl

Guests around

Self-esteem and self-love

Do not tell me

I fell in love

Your false face

I have got used to

Guests around

I do not pretend to

like me

Pigs are you all so staged - ugly TECHNOLOGY

Your love

We greatly understand

Indian painting in your face

Only lust and lust

You do not look decent hand

And ready for

We understand that you guys mind

That is the end of the bowl live thinking about pot

We are not afraid of you confess

We accompany just money

Please ask your conscience

I fell in love with a meal they said

Eat the next meal do not know who you love

If you love your family to hear such a bullshit

I do not know how she is sad and hate

Not you betray your lover's feelings

Is that you fooling us showgirl

At the same time you go against their conscience

What you get is destined only false

July 10, 2000

Words to my husband

Dear husband

For a long time I want to tell you

I was afraid to expose your game

It is hard to step down

We are embarrassed

What worries me is

We'll teach children how

We expect children to go much further than we

They want spiritual holiness

And their idols father

But outside mistresses

How can we preach the good children up to learn

My husband, I am not afraid to say to you

While your wife strongly with your performances

However, we can disguise was so perfect it

We can guarantee to keep the kids know the truth

If children know they are the most lovable father

In mistresses, raising Xiao Mi

How the child will have to face reality

They will not believe your most trusted father

It was such a bad guy

Often teach children to make progress, benevolent father

Actually hypocrisy, is immoral hypocrite

In the glorious image of the child

You kind of "good" father how dissimilar

We want our children to adult

To have a good home, a happy little family

We also hope that our adult daughter

You can upright Zuoren, by their own efforts married

Shame not to do wicked things, but not for other people's mistress,

We will not accept other people's own daughter for Xiaomi

Like other people's parents do not accept their daughter Xiaomi

Please dear husband

I hope you respect for law and morality

I hope you still have human nature and conscience

Do not hold other people's money to play with daughter

Others decidedly parents will not let you

Just like your daughter would not let people play with the same

Tell your husband, and was solemnly tell you

Below the belt carrying other people's parents,

God will not forgive you

Day of reckoning will come

Moral corruption husband

I used to not want to marry a man

Wife will hate you in grief and regrets

                                          August 10, 2000

Walking on the streets

Night without incident

Unmatched street

Impetuous things

Bear river

Laughing ass fucker

Vamp color women hug

Like Pig line step

Woman dragged fireworks

Surface mounted door play, self-deception

I do not know the truth but invaluable, easy to buy sensual

Strange Bedfellows, sectarianism

People ah people

Between good and bad only an idea

To obscene, degrading to

As easy as drinking water

                        2000 August 19 night

Living in this world

The chance to learn for 20 years

Travel ten years

Jun asked how obtained

Not in words only laugh

Rivers and lakes more sinister

Things difficult to predict

Gentleman Easy hegemony

Anti-Hypocrisy hardest

By fraternizing

Philistine who is attached Potential

August 25, 2000

It's hard to be the wife of poet

Wife

I tell you the truth

The reason I still happy living

All because of you by my side

Wounds of the past too much

Reality is cruel torment over me

In a secular society substances

Your husband will not kitsch poet

It is not secular favor

He hoped that in the spiritual realm

The only thing you can get is the husband of the poet's poems

As a poet's wife

You have to face reality

You will not opportunistic poet

He could not make a lot of money for your sleek profiteers

He did not so much energy to make money for you to live

In the dazzling life

He only your favorite poem

You can do the princess in his ideal kingdom poetry

But can not be too wide in the reality of material life

The poor poet

Others may not understand

The poet's sad

Others may not understand

As the poet's wife

You must learn to appreciate and taste husband

If you do not understand her husband's spiritual world

If you can not experience the same with her husband in the fun

Your husband is with strange bedfellows

Please forgive your husband's incompetence

Can not let you enjoy doing well

In today's real life

My dream in another world

                                                        2000 Mid-Autumn Eve

Father's love in the heart

I was sad for a long time

Is my daughter alone

This was no longer selfish selfish world

I was most pleased

It is my lovely and amiable daughter

Lost love I can not

There have been love I can bury

Unique my flesh and blood can not be separated

But what of the forsaken lover

Snobbish already got morals

Say the truth

For me, only the fatherly heart forever

The world's most pro-family is pinned in their flesh and blood body

The continuation of life is reflected in the body of the offspring

The most desirable is my darling daughter

September 25, 2000 Night

Feeling in the winter night

Everything passed

Calm as a mirror

Merry old things smoke without a trace

Sigh

It came among people sharing a bed with me

But now there are a bit exotic Ying

Think worth mentioning, worth mentioning love

The world situation as thin as paper

Only kinship long hanging heart

                         2000 November 24 Night

Helpless sad

I want to get angry

But, I am more of a frustration

Such is life torture

I have to endure the things I can not stand

I also must learn to endure the drag on

Laughing and crying are not the answer

Vent only sentimental own

God will seem helpless

I can only feel helpless sadness in silence in

January 23, 2001 years

Taste the woman

A woman is a man born stunner

If you have a good woman

You have to cherish and carefully taste

If you have a bad bad woman despicably

Then you simply prostituted themselves in

Regardless of how women have the capability

Women must first be our man's hope and sustenance

Women must be an indispensable element in a combination of family

No matter how great woman

Women must play the role of the Virgin and Eros

What woman is

Woman is our dream to conquer

           February 16, 2001

With my son, without love

Although the trouble with children

I resign

A taste of the joy of children

Now think about it: no children how unfortunate

Lost love and lost kinship compared

Nothing

Lost love: can endure, you can find

Loss of flesh and blood: unbearable, can not be replaced

You can dream of sustenance

Emotion may be grown in a suitable person

Love or marriage bundles available

Because God knows

In certain environments: Love has no choice

Love for burial

Unique flesh and blood family can not be separated

February 20, 2001

I think

I think

I really would like you to do any intimate action

Because your body is really attractive

Confuse taste my heart

I hug you are most willing to do

You see that innocent innocent

I was truly rejuvenate

Red heart and numbness of the shaking

Desire finally washed up

I think you can only be in my heart

Because I can not shirk its responsibility to shoulder

Including you and my family

I have to keep his nose clean

You just want a moment of instinctive impulse

Let alone love you

March 7, 2001

Living without the memory

Years will become beautiful or sad memories

Memories of old things. How

Only a bit sad, a bit helpless

Silent, independent thinking

Q. How God

Actually teach people eat tasteless, sleepless night

Red saying their love is the most harmful

Not as good as chest without distractions, random fugue

My body has no Buddha, no phyisal body

March 29, 2001

A crying man

I cry

I can not afford to support a family man crying

I cried not dare to be seen

My eyes are flowing tears disappointing incompetence

I can not run out of energy well breadwinner

I have racked their brains to make ends meet

My family burden is too heavy

I can only maintain the income of live

I cried, I cried afraid to let parents know old

Their ill and can no longer withstand the tough life

I cried, I cried afraid to let his wife know that sharing a bed

Like me, she

Like an exhausted old cattle dragging this heavy crawl home

I cried, I cried afraid to let children know

Child's childhood should be a better world

I cried, but I have to stir up the burden of life

I cried, but I have to assume household responsibilities

Family needs me, my parents, wife and daughter need

The main backbone of the family fail

Want to live in me sustenance

I secretly tears

I also like the daylight MAN

I know I'm vulnerable

I have to help the young and old love, went ahead following

I cast a quilt at night without the sound of tears

But during the day comforting smile wife

After always better, certainly better future life

Yet, who knows

I was crying! Amen

April 10, 2001

The feeling and life

Passion is over

Good times no longer returns

Let me try world-style first love

It has long been forgotten over time

But worldly love struggle

Like love lingering smoke no match for the wind

Only their console the wounds of

Life does not believe in tears

Marriage just believe reality

In certain social family

Motherhood may no longer need

Because maternal love match for selfish

This allows even more great Father

What is happiness

Happiness is the feeling of a better life

All good to be happy all the contents of humanity, love and selfless

Otherwise, happiness will become selfish, materialistic

Earthly inconstancy

Only experience will appreciate - how people are selfish and ruthless

Run into a loving but not related to the person you

You only have bad luck

Affection, caring and blood of people seem thicker than water

Selfish relatives

It appears strange kinship

We need affection

But, we need self-esteem

When our family so that when self-esteem is not guaranteed

We have to choose to give up family self-esteem

Because we can rely on self-esteem and alive

But we can not rely on family and live

There will always sour and sweet

God will never disappoint my efforts

Thank God

Wife is my own choice

I laugh in the end I met a woman

Cohabitation is no longer my choice

Marriage finally established in my will

World greatest good for nothing

Let your heart like a dog with a woman you

Amen!

May 27, 2001

People behave like Beer

Look at them

Bigger way

On a good dress

Right demeanor

People seem to noise shows

We are successful people

Who knows better representation

Once it is better to expose valuable pigskin

Hypocritical hearts and ugly face

Will show on the other side

God is good deception

Social conscience has been this big vat dye transfer numb

Fame is a human-like bear's Creed

August 21, 2001

Poet and pig

It was quite funny

A person engaged in Poetry

Actually, huh greasy cooked food to

Fortunately, he is upset

Well in order to survive

Involuntary

Do whatever

As long as self-reliant

What wronged embarrassed

Sixty-seven House

There's illiterate parents rarely live

Be under ignorance teach orphans

There are not assertive, not calendar event wife

My main backbone not try any of their hard leather

God will kill my family leather

What poet? Ass

Poetry can eat

I do not know really well-fed starving suffer

It is imperative to maintain family life

A seven food to eat

Often parents have medicine for the disease

Ignorant children have the chance to read

The greatest mission

Breadwinner

Yulong sing some words

Cry the old customers

Today's pig, pigtail, pig face how good

Golden color and delicious

Brother, you want to Lao Shu kilograms

Aunt, aunt you want a few two

I do not know how much goes bitterness of bitter tears

Zuoren ah, difficult

As the breadwinner men harder

Smiles greet

This is a lie to say that the court cuisine, ancestral production

How how to taste

It is nothing more than a few customers to sell more

Earn a few corners near good solution difficult

This technique is a businessman

But for people to write poetry I learned

It is a noble or despicable only God knows

August 25, 2001

The bad boss

Who says I can not hack shameless seven

I look back straight and bulging like the Boss

Line is the duck walk, take the chairs

Smoked imported cigarettes and drink foreign wine

And travel by car, there are blocks of residential

Although a wife, a good friend but a lot

To open a restaurant, near the government to do business

Wild species are geometry, is still mind

Speaking of family history

Thanks to learn bad

Set hair household

Pain people changing for the better

Money banks

Money to make money

A karate move

From scratch to set the wolf

Quasi tangible opportunities

Loans to natural

In the office can not do something in the wine on the table to do

Say a word during the day in the evening to say

Nothing mortgage took kickbacks to clear the way

Please, fawn, Pei Xiaolian

Caring, generous, heavy friendship

Silver bullet, together with bombers

Bank lending is not afraid

Afraid supervisor does not favor

Not enough money to get loans

To use funds on the cutting edge

Businessman's nature is for profit

The best high-profit catering

Opening a restaurant you have to find the background

What things are easy to handle

Restaurant hardware is good

But success in the software

Miss Mommy good training

Most diners tippler Italian

Red Edge Good Reception

Success is inevitable

Experts know a lot of tricky,

Others die Girl

Splenetic me far more than a shameless seven

Eat the bulk is still behind

                                        September 5, 2001

Feeling when I was sick

Although the hospital is a place of healing

But also burn stove

Doctors really bears the responsibility to save the Dead Fusheng

But also for the paid service

Remember that famous saying

There is no free lunch

Hospital shall so

Serving the People

But people here have to pay

You can not afford Restaurant

You can afford to go to the mall

But, you came to the hospital

You can afford to get sick

You can not have the money

You can cure somebody to help you pay

If you can not afford too sick sick

That is, your hapless relatives

If your loved ones can not afford or lack of filial piety

Ultimately bad or your own

Remember: disease-nice

Health is a blessing

How it is to cherish the body, a lot of care about their

September 21, 2001

The dream and life

As a 28 years old man

Busy working everyday

Get up early and run in the frog

Upload month stay late Ben dark village

A single shoulder livelihood

Rules of the game to make money hunt

Sleep dream party Dawu

Life is but a drama

Confused most of their lives

However, three meals a day seeking, seeking night night

How much sleep at night, but also house five feet high

Why bother to humbly ask for help

By his mother's gas

                                        September, 26,   2001

Don't be too bad to yourself

Life is life

Calm

Far more than a matter of injustice

Than my great injustice by its people

Calls out grievances

Only swallow

In certain segments of society

Only weak Gouqietousheng

Because: the weak no match for the powerful

Humble war but tyrannical

Where is justice

Although not necessarily in heaven with me

Sigh

The poor ghost is calling me

September 28, 2001

The miracle is caused by yourself

Vicissitudes of life

Painful

Inconstancy

Desperate nonsense

Ask the heavens earth

I believe this world who

Everyone selfish

All self-care

What is friendship, affection, love

Feeble

Legal Hao

Moral worth mentioning

This is not a god panacea

Materialistic world

Self-interest is the Almighty Spirit

Do you believe

God will not bless the poor

Only a savior

That's your own

Amen also unreliable

Buddhist monk

Long road Shinto even without words

Amitabha

Dead do not read a miracle

                                        October 13, 2001

Prosititute's heart

Good evening, Mr. shout loudly

It turns out I was greeted with a smile helpless heart

To meet you, I'm so happy

This is a lie to your story

You send a wink

In order to retain the business

Strange guests left

Strange guests again

Send hypocrites

With passenger zombie

Sound good to go, you devil management

Send money plague, trans people do not recognize the face

Then the rich boss

The money can only buy meat

Inability of the heart

How can the old regular customers

Miss nature

Rich boss, money bastard

This lady is not interested in conscience to say

There is a saying

Heartless bitch, actors nonsense

I have the ability

I love flirting expert

They lie lies lying

I had inadvertently

Early in my heart to make guests tuning numb

He said Mr. loudly, Hello confused

Curse you one: idiot idiot

Savvy not you

Love you with money wishful thinking

Since ancient times

Loaned money to people, but the night his wife

Prostitutes only meat, never pledge allegiance

                                          The evening of 14 October 2001

Repentance of the heart

Relationships

In fact, it is to achieve a net individual utilitarianism

Whether you admit it or not

Society in the post friends

Most are utilitarian friends

Friends need to take care of each other

Use of each other is a very common technique

For the kind of pure friendship dating has been away from us

Our world is no longer pure spirit

Pollute our souls by too many

Holy soul is no longer captive

We need to repent of our original soul

Holy soul we need to apologize for our early drop dead when

We need not all materialism and irritation

We must also support the need to empty the soul of conscience

We are human beings

If we have a point, then humanity

Please repent for their sins

Please repent for their dark side

We are doing our conscience make life difficult thing

How can we ask others to do honest man

Each person to society for too long

I must apologize for my soul

If you're really a little bit of conscience, then

That apology bar

Please take a repentant apology friends

                              October 15, 2001

Pray for my dead dog

Pain in the heart is still thinking of you for years

My dear white dog

The world's most loyal friend

That terrible disease so you never away from me

He taught me to live alone human infinite sadness

Draw a conclusion

Your life is written eternal loyalty

You are never too poor spiritual master never let mankind admire

A four-legged loyal friend

Much better than the snobbish friends feet

Vicious people

Let me emotional

Materialistic relationships let me chilling despair

You miss and get along very happy day indeed

That Qinmi seamless intimate life makes me happy to be happy

Select Comfort never have a good day

Leaving only your infinite pain and nostalgia

Your graves green to yellow

Only my heart still worried about your

My good white dog

Friends sharing weal and woe of the world's most

I pray to God for you

Meeting in the afterlife, life and death never pay

I think of you all the good

Past has emerged in front of the good old days

Really time I see a dog heart

Trouble now True Friends

Good guys harder and harder dog in humanity

You let me through thick and thin since I was very sad

Tears his face

Objectively speaking

Spirituality is not just a good dog dog

In addition to the performance of their friend or friends

Dog is so faithful to the Lord's humanity and goodwill

The life of some people is better than a dog has become

October 18, 2001

Cannot live like this anymore

I have seen in the car robber robbery

The people in the car are not dared argue

Including me

I have seen mob violence on the street

And all the people in the street to avoid

Including me

I have seen the thief steal the food market

No one dared to stand up for justice in the market

Including me

We have to timid as a mouse

Our smart numb

We have cold cold heart pumping

Our conscience has long been eating Tengu

We have the courage to protect themselves conquered

We face is not conducive to their own thing indifferent

We dare to stand face to face evil anti-Doo

We are left with no conscience and human body

We left the flippancy of demands and desires

We are left with is cowardly cowardice

Why do we live such a wimp
Why do we live so selfish
Why are we afraid to live injustices say
We lack the courage to not only conscience
We lack not only the power of well integrity

We have to dare to recognize our own self-protection
We calculate that even conscience are counted out
We no longer have to live personality and integrity
We live like rats like disgrace

We are living in the end for what
In addition to fame, money and pleasure outside
Also in the end what we should strive for and stick
Whether life should live so selfishly
We really do not have to just kind heart and the soul of integrity
We need solidarity and good cooperation we are really sincere
Because: We have two to tango
Because: Separate the weak force strong match for evil
We need joint efforts to safeguard social justice
We need to maintain good social environment

Alive not just for themselves

Alive not just for food and shelter and a small family

We are alive and need Chardonnay colors and selfless devotion

We are alive and need our spirit and conscience to support

We dare not confront injustice

How can we joke about life and ideals

Things we are afraid to face their own

How can we be so hypocritical to educate our next generation

Do an ideal, as a man of integrity

October 19, 2001

The life doesn't believe tears

Despite the hardships of life

Gotta be the day too

We have reason to abandon illusions

We have no reason to give up life

No matter how hard suffering in the face of adversity

Gotta be taken forward pace

Now that sounded the horn of life

Racing living spaces can not quit

We can only survive in advance

We will not flinch in the shelter may have

Only from time to time in the wheel of life turn

Family expenditure will decidedly not stop

We only have a way of life efforts and hard work

Different to heaven a big pie is the most unrealistic thing

Remember: we are lucky few civilians

We only have to pay the sweat and toil to survive and live

October 23, 2001

The sad tears in the dream

Midnight Dream crying sad

Tears flooded inconstancy

Helpless, helpless

Shen Jie lonely life want anything else

Tropsch put things on the Night's Dream

And had to tell

Still unknown

October 28, 2001

The wine for the wine ghost

Ugh

Who bitterness and a belly

But only toast words "wine ghost"

Only the wine can eliminate the worry

Cups after cups

Li Bai even sober

Drunk and made his poem

I do not come, etc.

Come regret it

Like the wine for the ghosts

One thousand drunk party

Because drop of wine spiced taste

Mention color embolden

And drinkers create the world

The "alcoholic" wine accompanied

Why fear the opponent peers

                      November 27, 2001

We must bite the bullet

I'm a man who told

A man must bite the bullet

Big burden somehow tam

Then a big responsibility must also be borne

If the sky is falling down

Men have to withstand

Our families need us weak men Tiedan steel shoulder

A person's hopes are pinned on us to men

Jagged man

Own tears flow

It is a strong sense of responsibility of man

Please put all the responsibility for taking on himself

Only those soft egg

Those students who do not have a weak "lifeblood" of

Wife will hide behind the man escape responsibility

Cry day

Our broad mind can hold the world hardest difficult

He calls out to

Our shoulders are strong enough to carry the burden of the world

Perseverance in the face of adversity

Pain in bear

Man is a hero

Not afraid of difficulties and obstacles

Fear of failure setbacks

Caring bloody man

Please protection and care in the plight of our good small family

Because: We need our men to care for his wife and daughter care

Amen

November 30, 2001

Destiny of the poet

When I realized

I have become a real poet when

I am no longer self

As long as the beating heart sinking poetry

I can only belong to poetry

In the world of poetry

Everything must give way to poetry

Although difficult life can be all sorts of suffering I

However, a hard life but can not take the joy when writing poetry

Writing poetry can be derived from life experience

Beautiful poem, but only from the genius of inspiration

Selfish person

Although you can not change poet

But the poet's heart

Not for the fame and fortune away Battle

Life may force the poet tears down

But life is not forced to concede defeat Poetic yield

Although sometimes unreasonable to tell this world

Poetic justice, but it can tell its own

In the materialistic society

Although things can sometimes distort reversed

However, the world of poetry

Receiving only good and beautiful

The poet can endure all the suffering in society

People can also live up to the poet

The poet does not have any reason to live Poetic

The poet does not belong to his own himself

The poet does not belong to his own small family

The poet first part of the poem

The world belongs to poetic inspiration

Poetry

Poet's soul

Poetry

God is the poet

Poetry

The poet's dream and future

Poetry

Where is the spirit of the poet

Poetry

In the eyes of others

It can be ass

Poems can

In the eyes of the poet

But it is immortal panacea

It is a source of courage and unyielding

Poetry

You can heal the soul of a poet

Poetry

You can forget the evil people

Poetry

You can enhance the poet's righteousness

Poetry

You can clean the poet heart and soul

To Poetry

The poet can betray love

To Poetry

Poets can leave their homes

To Poetry

The poet can even betray family

Whether or not people understand

Poets and poetry must be scheming

The poet was born not for himself

The poet is not live for yourself

The poet must write poetry alive

Write earth selfishness can not write poetry

Write poetry on earth the fairest and most sincere heart poetry

        February 1, 2002 in Beiliu

        February 3 2002 revised in Yulin

There will be the last day of the evils

Human insidious

Than to set up a trap in front of

And then told you to jump

Human vicious

Than threatening evil

Then people behind the sale

The most frustrating thing

Than knowing that this had to whom

I do not want to do their own thing

Forced their conscience trained

The pain and frustration only their own experience

Help people made a scapegoat

Only dumb to suffer in silence

Regulation people

Because Dances with Wolves

Behind the Smile

But it is harboring evil intentions

Ugh

Sigh

It is not for my own personal

I am not really evil wish

Vicarious time will not be long

Act as Wrigley day there will always be one at the end

Ancient couplet in my conscience freed

Determined to do good, although not good reward

Unmotivated evil, evil though no penalty

                        February 23, 2002

After dead

Died after

Soul ceases to exist

Speaking after any dead

Or heaven see God

Hades or hell will

It is disrespectful to the dead

Families of injustice

In fact, later died

Stop thinking it

Send this soul body no longer exists

Speaking after any dead

Also wandering soul heaven

Or still wandering the world

Fool all of the dead

Of living fraud

Reality though so speechless dead

Let acting in nonsense

Let science sometimes powerless

Living as we

Should death of the deceased

And the dead can not be confronted with our protest

What nonsense it's cause and effect of good and evil

What nonsense or heaven or hell like a lie

Any spiritual cultivation

And how to be pious Bong

We can not have God may be summoned

In fact, my master does not exist

Channel, believers can not change the fact that nothingness

Although science can later confirmed dead souls will no longer exist

But science was unable to persuade people no longer believe in God

If you die after the soul really exist

Our ancestors did not know the number of dead

All corners of life should be filled with the spirit of their ancestors

We are free to reach out and touch the souls of their ancestors

The truth is, we do not touch the soul

No! Then the fact that proof

After the dead, the soul is gone

Any sustenance afterlife say

Chedan are nonsense words

Are baseless superstition is strong-minded

I want to deceive the world Road priests, monks

I can say the truth

Treat the dying person should not continue to deceive

Sadly enough the dead

Say it conscience

Soul will be with you

God definitely can not forgive the soul deceive people

Our lives from natural

We will also return to nature after death

God created any discourse

Are the parents of ingratitude

Negative natural justice

April 4, 2002

Don't believe the writers

Writers hypocrisy

As the pen hypothesis

Although the wonderful text

Although the plot moving

It is also a false story

Hateful writers

Then at its false garland

Originally some ugly soul

As some celebrity as

Glorious image can not cover up its ugly soul

Although the work can support the false appearance of Scholars

Sun Life was able to restore the author's face

As some singers, movie stars, like

Stage star who can bring out the charm of gold

However, it has exposed the original face under shadowless lamp life

Do not believe Scholars

Like I do not believe in stars, actors as

Live like a normal person like

With a normal heart

It's better than what worship

Amen

                                                                May 11, 2002

The song for my thirties

Thirty men bent bow

They can not help themselves and could not itself

Living like a clock-like

Did not cease progressively

Although the prime thirties

Helpless consume too large

To be under the care of the old and the young pity

There also need to comfort his beloved wife

Innocent children have been placed

Early juvenile vision belongs

Passion is the abundance of its heyday when they were young

Prime responsibilities and obligations under the shoulder

Ugh

Sigh

How much emotion into the brave brawny

Also no time embrace his wife

July 8, 2002

Hard to find the right person

Talk with press

Like in the food market as easy to find a greengrocer

Get Publishers

Like as difficult to grandmother

Difficulty is encountered difficulty discerning publisher

I can endure loneliness

I can endure loneliness

I can live on lonely Creation

There are hardships in life

But, I can not stand the most is published on the pathless

The burden of life has made me do a depleted

Creative soul even more painstaking

My heart is crying

My creative soul in shock

I can create the best poem

However, I was unable to launch the work in front of the reader

Because: In any country where the legal publishing

Publishing is beyond the control of our creators wish

Although the publisher is not cute but still have to find

Although strong publishers hate but better late than never

Although rare earth discerning Bole

I retreat but no

I can not publish my good work

I can only be buried in the vast sea of people

Can the good work put in front of the reader

Only a day alerted

"Joy of God" can launch

Only a discerning publisher dared to define

And if I'm lucky encounter Chen Jinyong

Only after the joy of success is to face emotion

It's hard to find the people who recognize your ability

August 5, 2002

Quack - helpless poet

In my life

The poet is not selected

Holy mind can not dominate the reality of life

Abundance also lost soul on material deprivation

Health and Living

Not just what the poet himself

As a husband and a father who's a poet I

There is no reason simply my personal own

Ideal for any creative lifestyle

Are elusive things

I have one thousand reasons to put down the pen

But not a reason not to take on the task of raising a family

Because: I do not there are people Creation Creation

I do not support their families, who breadwinner

Law and morality, conscience and human nature

Let me have a million reasons to let family had to live

Life is like a devil threatening evil

As no business quality and no special skills I

Can live has been very good

And then to take care of the sick, the elderly and young children

It is a very difficult

Just think of home firewood, rice, salt, oil running out

They have not created the desire

Beautiful poem again only buried in the soul

Then good verse only aborted

You can stop for a nice poem

Can calmly reflect on your own creations even better

Can for me it really is a dream

Life is like hungry dogs running around the same force poet

Business people to get rich

The poet is to do business breadwinner

God calls out

Why call injustice I met

Both the poet as a fruit vendor

Laughing service for selling fireworks are denounced

But also for the rain on the street selling watermelons

Complain the pain as "Watermelon Song"

Butcher cooked longer term pain sing Yulong Song

Now it becomes charlatans boast sell wine

Really Sopranos Shenbuyouyi

Since ancient times, poets suffering

No amount of suffering only wine and song

The soul does not require people to have a special worship substance

I hope those people who bought my wine

God bless: After effects such as elixir

Long as the rivers in the poet so I can feel at ease some children

                      October,3, 2002 in Yulin

                      October 5 2002 revision

The small family and love

I think he is wise

Every day, put on a mask and armor out of melee

But I wonder if someone like me

Even the best masks and armor can not protect our hearts

Scarred hearts are bleeding every day

Lonely desolate souls floating around

In this materialistic society

Small home is the most memorable and comforting haven

The most pro-favorite is our own family

In this small house

Mind to be purified and rinsed

Soul sincere treatment and proper care

Hypocrisy is not on our face painted write

False heart vanished without a trace

Cry relatives ah

This small home is our beloved earth

Sigh soul

That is our ultimate spiritual anchorage

No fighting out here

In this holy mind guaranteed

                        November 18, 2002

Sank helpless

I have seen enough of the world's hypocrisy

I see the world's crafty

I'm tired of the world's sinister

I see tired people desire

And cunning villain along

Like thousands of ants bite body as uncomfortable

And as both prostitutes and Li Ching of Signs of acquaintance

Such as the swallow flies like a sick and

Hypocrite hypocrisy

Not only for people who can not become king

The world's shameless

Since that is ugly but also gild

Worse

Hypocrisy is always hiding behind the insidious

This is very hard to make honest man

The rest is

I sympathize with those who scapegoat the poor Scapegoat

More people sigh is

Why should the sheep in front of the wolf wolf-like divisions

Honest people ah

Heart black enough, evil enough heart, enough poison heart

This doomed

Good man wronged, out of the way of the wicked

Vulnerable people deserve sympathy and pity

May under certain circumstances

But also helpless helpless

Cry Amen

Bale only look out for themselves

                          November 20, 2002 in Beiliu

Make poem

When people get to make poets and poetry pomp

This has been the vulgar ostentation

Elegant poetry is not attached to the wind can taste

Beautiful poem is by no means everyone can understand

Beautiful soul of poetry only know Salon

Poetry is not public programs - everyone Fun

Poetry, nor is it a clown or comic - let everyone laugh

Poetry, but not video or song - make people pleasure red

Poetry is elegant, fine art is the soul

Poetry, not everyone can do, can be written in the holy soul

Do not mess poetry

Chaos poetry is poetry does not respect

But also for their ignorance mockery

World Poetry does not allow horseplay

Poetry is not allowed between heaven and earth have desires

Poetry, unlike fiction - can concoct

Poetry, unlike film - real ones

Poetry, it's not like your arable land - something in return

Poetry, poetry in the world can not hold the slightest false pay

Poetry, poetry in the world to accommodate the truth and holiness

Do not make fun of poetry

Otherwise, poetry rage against your ignorance in verse

I want to read poetry, to poetry products

Please read with a pure mind

Please bare atrium product

Do not take the slightest worldliness

                        November 22, 2002 in Beiliu

Part II: God Poet

Live, live for the clean souls

Do not put off for a few dollars and fancy

Youth has been excessive wear and tear

It should belong under Love yourself

The others live too tired

Comfortable living for themselves when it can now

The poor are our own

We like a robot-like busy

But do not know for yourself should be casual

Do not value their own lives to pay

It is to disregard the value of life

To know

We are born not just live for others

We must live for their freedom

We lived for others

Not only because of the love and compassion

There are social customs and conventions of collateral consanguinity

We live for yourself

Not only because of the desire and freedom

But also because we need to know

Why do we live

How should we alive

Alive, tiring

Not normal to live way more annoying

Too tired body should rest

Excessive cardio should purify contaminated

Too twisted soul should be corrected

We should reproduce the original face

Evil and right and wrong are not we supposed to have

Cunning and apathy is not our original nature

The Holy Spirit is not our greed and treachery hearts

We call not only our original goodness

We call the original and our conscience

Alive

Please for myself

For their own peace of mind alive

For their clean soul alive

Even if just for one day

November 27, 2002

An ordinary heart with aimbitions

Look at the cold world

Unpredictable things and difficult people

But also ambitious pride Trinidad

How God can tolerate this

It shabby poverty to fear

More independence pen Glyph heart

Poor's not my fault

Rich is not my dream

Bread and water leisure day

Chang E cloud drive will write

Hi nor music

Worry worry Yimo

Has turned the fortunes of the world

How to control his situation

Bearish Life

Jun worry own poetry Solutions

November 28, 2002

Be good to your life

Do not hurt anyone's self-esteem

Even if his position is more humble

As long as he has an unyielding desire to do better

Perhaps there will be a stone recovers

Let it be equal to forgive others

Warning anyone in the world by people who send away

If your instigation evil intentions

In respect of any human evil day stop

Sale to help people made a scapegoat is the most bad business

Vicarious scapegoat is the most let the world the object of ridicule

Shenbuyouyi day should end

Conscience and conscience should recall

Giant motives for the measurement of dedicated people most worth

Worldly way out ten million

Freedom to live the most important

Recruit ten million ways to make money

Live only for himself one stroke

Give up desire, heart with nature

The lines of their own

Do not oppress the oppressed people you can

And people will consume their fight for a better life

Precious time spent on boring self-injury phase from evil

It is the most stupid fool

I wish good heart

God will punish evil souls

                                                        December 9, 2002

Miss the dog

Rereading Dog Poetry

Miss the dog hurtfully

Who knows the meaning of the poet

The dog is little but left us

There's no language can expresss the poet's heart

A normal person like me

Far away from good education background

Please be far away from poetry

See the hungry village women are laughing

                              December 21, 2002

Misfortune and happiness

Nothing to do

Friends gather

See the escorts together

Eating the home cooking for long time

Wildflowers' tastes provoke heart

Insight into the state of prostitution

Men lust

Heartless whore

Clients like pigs

Heart rotten as feces

Looks like a gentleman

Fair without

Sex before

Like animals such as livestock

Pity pity people

Shameless degrading

Act like a buffoon

Pigs and dogs than

We advise the world

Food color for men and women

Abstinence

Thriving

December 22, 2002

Reading in the cold night

Raining winter night

Cold day deserted dilute

Return to the hosue made from mud

Hot wine poetry reading

December 25, 2002

Seeking the lost poet heart

I know

Why is it difficult now to get good poetry published

I know

Why good poetry cannot be published easily

The former, how difficult published poetry

Because too many people spoil poetry

Put a little more shit also called poetry

Ruined so that people can not read the point

Now add little poems sales

Few shocking good poetry

Talk about the immediate short term profits encounter publishers

Even the best poems will die dead pull pull

The latter, not a good poem Why publishing easy

All because the author is a "rich" who have

Only the rich afford the publishing charge

Or it is inextricably with the publishing industry hotshots off Shito

The garbage has been able to publish poems

All because the editor and publisher of self-interest and Hunyu

We are looking for the right publisher

We shall call the conscience and poetic

We look forward to good poetry

We have to look forward to good editor and publisher of integrity

We lost not only poetry, Poetic

We lost more poetic feeling and responsibility

Seek to take its place without being to editors

We must loudly scolded earthquake

In its wake indifferent knitting heart

World of good works can not be published

As the editors of the management feel ashamed and guilty

We call not only publish institutional reforms

We call for a more poetic heart

December 26, 2002

The clean souls and the poem

People forget Poetry

Poetry is not just their own reasons

Perhaps the outside world better than poetry

Diversity and social development

Sensory stimulation is always stronger than the feelings of art

Desires and interests of the people only allowed to deter death

Elegant poetry need to have high quality of spiritual experience

The only thing to be vulgar vulgar soul

Poetry is no longer a public thing

Poetry is just some people's hearts Inner Voices

Poems do not need more readers

Poetry will only need to taste the taste of her people

Poetry is no longer what fame

Poetry of her own unique content quality

And she can taste the holy man must be spiritually

Any person in possession of self-interest will not taste the holy Poetry

Many of the world may be able to rely on violence

The Poetry taste

Poetry has only holy soul

April 24 2003

Read Poem and do nothing

Seen through the ways of the world

Cup of tea might slow

Read a good poem on

Bad breath and dirty to clean belly

Purification of the mind for a long time by the secular assimilation

Meditation heart without seeking to Ning

An air and calm the soul before

Burial crazy desire

Abandon the pursuit of worldly

And true stop

Really serious reading on a high state of poetry

With the noblest poetic soul conversation

Maybe you'll get back your original nature and conscience

                      2003 4-29 Night

Lie down to see and knee down to read

When you see a good novel

You can look at lying

Because: This may be a sweet dream dashed

When you read a good poem when

You must read knees

Because: you may be a noble and poetic soul conversation

2003 4-29 Night

Who is doig evil on the street

Do not sympathize with poor street beggars

They cheated us not just money

They cheated us and also present good conscience

We are ignorant of their alms

We do not know in front of the so-called generous

Actually real endless fraud

They mocked us not just simple ignorance

They mocked us and our wisdom and kindness

Cheat a little technology can deceive us all goodness

We will be able to deceive people disoriented good

This is sad or funny

Not a clever little lie TECHNOLOGY

You will be able to deceive the good people of money and kindness

A false show can deceive people mercifully

Our conscience can not help trembling

Who fraudulently took our money in debauchery

Who fraudulently took our money in eating and drinking

Who is unconscionable to spend this money

Good people who drink blood

We can not help but ask

This in the end who is evil

This in the end who is buried conscience

Deceive human goodness

Deceive the good people of compassion

God in heaven will be cursed: Damn

This is unconscionable to spend money that really hacked in pieces

Make fun of people's kindness would have been burned by lightning

Deception retribution will eventually come

I advise poor beggars size

Do not deceive the good people of charity

It is in the dry matter Duanzaijuesun

Trample humanity Charity

This is the evil doing bad

Take this unconscionable money

Ancestors are thought scandalous wicked

Good fool

Generations have tarnished

2003 4-30 Night

The nake poem heart

Sincere than poetic heart on the world

A true poet

Its work must be absolutely naked

Regardless of how language poets of exaggeration

The core has to be sincere poetry

Although the poet and his sometimes selfish

The poet's life

Although, like ordinary people, as the owner of property

May poet in the works

But requires absolute sincerity

Only naked Poetic

The main theme is poetry

Only naked Poetic

Yong is singing tone poems

in life

The poet can live like normal people

Even the poet can be as deceptive as a liar

However, in the works

The poet has to be absolutely sincere

The poet has to be absolutely naked

Because: Only the naked poetic heart

You can move yourself and others

Because: Only the naked poetic heart

To make poetry becomes sacred sublimation

Because: only naked Poetic

To make the poets and poems become eternal

Therefore, even if the poet has little evil in life

The poet also in the works to be absolutely sincere

Because: Only the naked poetic heart

To make poetry acquire eternal vitality

Because: Only the naked poetic heart

To make poetry the highest perfection

Only the world naked poetic heart can not deceive the

Because, I am a poet

I am a true and absolute poet

2003-5- 1 Monring

The pure poet

We really are a poet

But we are people first

Is the difference between man and the poet's place

We the people of the poem

Poet order to survive in today's society

The poet must survive the mass mentality

Any Poetic Soul

Can not dominant in battle substance

Poetry can not thrive in any physical competition

Whether ancient or modern poet poet

Regardless of how it was poetry

In all fairness, there are a few lucky ones

Society does not sympathy distressed poet

Society also does not poor talented poet

Because: human nature is selfish, the reality of society is beyond the control of our personal wish

The poet is not possible to survive beggar-like image

Although the poet gave all soul

Although poetry also rinse the crowd's hearts

The poet can survive if you want to lose face

Poets must live with the mentality of ordinary people

The world is such

Most precious would most worthless way of unpaid grants

God's people will not be held poet

Because: God equally unsympathetic talented poet

The difference between poetry and poetry is the record

Poetry who might just write a sentence

And who is creating poetry in his soul cries

Many people write poetry

Creative people rarely Poetry

Poetry is the number of people who speak and speed

And people talk about creating poetry is poetry soul

People talking about poetry with desire

And people talk about creating poetry is absolutely spiritual

People think they write poetry is poetry

Poetry and Creative people think they are afraid of is to create Poetry

all in all

Poet, whether written or invasive with soul

When the poet to write poetry or poetry in record time

The poet's state of mind must be absolutely poetic

Personality his creation of the poet must be absolutely sublime

Poet, poetry must also be a living soul

Because: only the soul of poetry is the most pure poetry

Because: only poetry is the soul of a poet has recognized the eyes of poetry

2003-5-6

The asking from the heart

We need such hypocrisy alive.

So we have to do with people wearing masks

If we no longer live so hypocritical

If we are no longer dealing with people wearing masks so

We will be the kind of life

Our life will be what kind of situation

Will we run into snags everywhere

Will we live very wimp

Our life situation will be like situation

We can not help ourselves

We only live to survive it hypocritical

We only have a day in order to protect themselves and their families to live with it

Yes, society is complex

Yes, we live in an environment variable and is always fraught with danger

Yes, our environment is occurring everywhere in the sinister heart

We can not help ourselves

Is this the reason we are alive hypocrisy

Is this what we masked the real reason for contact

If this is the case

We had our own sad and disappointed

We have to feel sad and disgust for our own way of life

This is not what we expect of life

This is not what we want living environment

This is not what we are looking for more interpersonal

So, who is forcing us to live against one

So, who is forcing us hypocritical dealings

Our selfish hearts

Our desire is endless soul

Our living environment itself

Or our human desires and consistently filled with sinister

I am puzzled

People are really unpredictable

Or the mentality of our lives is not normal

Our living environment is full of fish, ranging from high and low culture quality

Or our living environment there is only their own interests, there is no human selfishness

I can not help but gasped

Do we really prepared for life magic

Is it really a philosophy of self-preservation guidelines for our interaction with others

Do you think we will have to live every day of hypocrisy

Is it so that we have every day with people wearing masks to

This is too sad

People ah people

People live there Sha significance to this

Live Is Better Than Live

That no one could do

But our conscience

Our soul where to go

Our holy mind where to go

We as human beings should have gone kindness

We can no longer be so hypocritical alive.

We can no longer wearing a mask like that with people you

We might ask ourselves the conscience

We might feel the existence of our own conscience

We also wish to look at our own tortured soul

2003-5-15

The forever support

We are fooling ourselves

We deceive ourselves

Do you believe

When we are juggling

When we do business

When we have to achieve a certain purpose

We might say some ambiguous words

We not only deceived the other party

We fooled and our own conscience

for money

Many of us are betrayed conscience

For the benefit of

Many of us are unscrupulously plundered

To Greed

Many of us are struggling to chase

This is not just a game of survival

This is not just a rule of life

This may or Jingmai soul trick

This may or trampling slaughterhouse mind

We slaughter our own conscience

We may not feel pain

We discredit our own souls

We may not feel shame

We deceive our own hearts

We may not feel lost

Because: We have become accustomed to numb

Because: Our conscience has been buried for too long

Because: Our soul has been drifting away from us

We may just have left money and body empty

Blush can perhaps only for our poet

We are the walking dead

The poor can we have not yet,

We're soul to a dead end

Sadly, we can continue the way forward

We ran to the soul being decapitated career

We can still ignorant darkness applauded for their actions

We grabbed a lot of money to steal music

It may be too "smart" we have lost childhood innocence

Our conscience gone

Our conscience gone

Our soul where to go

Our humanity gone

All go to heaven yet

Or is gone to hell

People gain conscience of whoever the hell

And "stupid" for the poet but selfish people Evocation

The poet is not only to save the human conscience

The poet was also to save the soul

I want to ask

Let us live with many substances simultaneously

Life is really going to let us lose a holy soul

When people will not go against their conscience and willingness to do things

When it can rejuvenate people should regain their past innocence

If we can give up some of life have

We might be able to have some eternal things to make spiritual support

2003-5-20

Speak for the death

    Now that the receipt of the notice of death

    Any relatives are crying irreparable parting of the deceased

    The souls of the report is the natural corollary of

    Death arrangement who can not refuse

    Resistance may allow doctors to obtain a temporary victory

    The development of science can not let life forever

    Death is always a thing of the all creatures have to face

    The spark of life is always limited flash

    Can have the opportunity to continue its fate will depend on good fortune

    Please stop the pro-people sad

    Tears and affection touched only living

    Leaving life has its own causal reason

    Emotional human responsibility

    Revenant is meaningless in terms of

    Scores alive when this has been written off

    Do not cry so much

    All friends and relatives

    Another sad thing only man alive to bear

Kuma or blame the dead to no avail

No amount of tears flow of a deceased person is superfluous

Any Pimadaixiao, weeping practice

Students who are self-posturing of self-deception performances

Because: filial not by death with tears and expressions to act out

Filial need lifetime of real sincere treatment

Investigated the deceased's own causal retribution of good and evil

A Way to Hell

For his lifetime of evil must be the gate of hell

Perpetrators of crime is bound to ditch his lifetime repentance in hell

Soul will also be rinsed away from the world of torture

Somewhere, God will give a fair deal

The road to heaven

During his lifetime for the good of those who might be a blessing

But the troubles of the world

Soul or get permanent peace in paradise

Pro-life people treat

End of life is a natural thing

Life mission because people will not change

Sad, nostalgia

Only those who are born of unrequited love

Any farewell ceremony or memorial meeting

We are living for the living to see

The dead do not know it

No simple farewell ceremony is perhaps the wishes of the deceased

For extraordinary general deceased person

Consumers consume a lot of money in any way mourners

They are stupid, ignorant behavior of sin

Too much bother souls

It is the irony of living, the dead torture

Excessive hair dead money behavior

It will be subject to God's curse

People have lost loved ones

one way or another

Your loved ones, after all, has been away from you

This also allows the spirits of the dead givin

Since you want to leave quietly

With respect their wishes

Quietly let the road

For the living

The most sensible approach is to restrain their grief, take care of themselves

Because: the living must live

Tomorrow the sun will rise from the east

Of hope will reproduce

Change things might be able to build our human self-improvement

2003-6-5

Our spiritual homeland

Life has become so vulgar noble souls

Make money noble character becomes degrading

The challenges of survival people involuntarily

Alive responsibility not only for their own

Helpless is a true portrayal of our Lives

Average people do not need noble soul

Needless humble little need noble personality traits

Ordinary sentient beings talk about the immediate short term profits

Tangible benefits

Yong is the most public faith in God

Please do not talk with people of different paths

Different ways, not with seeking also

This is the old saying saying

Please do not discuss with people on a different level

Different levels, different views

This is a parody of howling at the moon

Dispute can only be resolved vulgar things

Communication needs of the soul without noisy claimed

Noble soul must stand in the outer mediocre mentality

Materialistic hearts of the people in need without re-sublimation of the spirit level

Do not talk about your idea of yearning and the people around you

It was an extraordinary spirit world

It is not the ideal situation for everyone imagined

And it is not everyone understands or longing for spiritual paradise

Because: The world does not belong to them

Because: The world belongs to us idealist

Because: a world that is drifting away from reality in the world.

Because: a world that is free from any social class dominated world

The world will be forever in our hearts

Although life becomes so difficult or heavy waste

Also under the mask even though we live every day in thousands of

Also let us play what role in society

Our spiritual home always worthy of our longing for life

It was a quiet soul over the world

It is expected to be one of only poets and poets paradise

2003-8-13

Easy to sell meat, hard to sell poem

People sell pork Peking University outstanding student

Pretty card is linked to the real stuff

As is the high value-added

Even the dignified genius

Chop bone carving exhilaration

And I "Ambassador" Ni Tuizi Sale poetry

With the only genuine poetry

FIG is homegrown

Even stray afar streets

Planing poetry but also cut heart swallow

November 11, 2005 to see reporting Peking University students felt while selling pork

2005-11-11

The poet and writer

The poet would like to make good poems

The first need is sincere

Only sincere poems will have the opportunity to win the reader's resonance

Writers want to create a good novel

The first need is to deceive

Only a bizarre plot story will attract more readers to read

This doomed

Most readers of the writer but not a poet

Because: People tend to think of the kind of self-deception masturbation feeling

The poet is unable to give

2005-11-21

The gambler's fate is upon himself

When greed and gambling when we want to control

We lose not only money and possessions

We also lost the conscience of humanity and should have

If we escape the greed of human nature

We may also escape the fate of this gambling portal

We want something for nothing did dream of getting rich

Really will put us stuck with bookmakers established rules of the game

And this gambling rules

For us gamblers it is undoubtedly a death sentence ruling

Everyone knows what the money was the fastest

Gambling no doubt some people preferred doorway

This option is available to participate in our own dealer under the knife

Adverse gambling regulations determine our ultimate tragic outcome

Not lose lose lose everything is no humanity

TIPS persons

Perhaps just a point to eat the loss and left the man-eating trap

Greedy person

There the fate of other people losing

In this unfavorable rules of the game

Makers are always afraid of the big gamblers winning

Just do not be afraid of gambling

As long as gamblers bet down

Gamblers outcome is self-evident

We want to win

Can anyone not want to lose

We want to win time

Why do not we think about we lose coveralls have turned, however, when

After losing remorse is of no use crying phase

Tears of regret will only make greed deserve mockery

No one among the world believe gamblers

Because: the conscience of humanity and gamblers have long lost in heaven

Gambler faces lined only fraud and greed

To save ourselves

To get people to believe us

We want to get our dream again dignity

Our first priority is self-respect, self-esteem, self-love

Rely on others to borrow money to change the fate of our people gambling

That idiot dream fantasy fairy tale

Change our destiny is the only option

Leave this bet does not win casino gaming establishments

But away from the greedy cunning Makers

Fangui ordinary people hard but without seeking mentality

November 20, 2005 in the north

2005-11-20

For my wift Aying

Wife ah

You are not wanted in nearly foot but far away

He said you do not love the poetry but selling action in the cold

Want you,

Although mouth

But I can only tell you in my heart

Love Your Heart

While you are still dancing

But also because of the scene in front of the deserted you love nothing

Today's business reality deserted

Elsie and people really read poetry not appear

Although many people were watching

But also I just like to have me as a clown

I have to say stupid, and I'm crazy Wealth

Epilepsy guys have made an idiot sold poem

More Road eternal anecdote sell only poet to play

Ugh! Laughter lean, but not laughing prostitute

How many ugly no one to Rage

Poetry crazy for Muse

Whimsical only people out to sell Chen dead poetry

Wife ah

Although I thought sell their own poems make some money to live

Who knows when the wind changed early

I could not help day wish

Today people want to hear is kill the pig squealing

I do want to see naked water creeping Sheban

But these "fine" acting

It is not the best husband

My husband is the ability to write a few poem

Doudou wife Joy

Since fool Ying-hi

However, in today's society benefits

But the majority of readers can not deceive the masses

Because: today this dream has long been unfashionable poetry is not the actual line of business

Even the best poems of people not rare

Several talented poet only dead pull pull dead

Perhaps poetry is the industry is too old

How old-fashioned spiritual resonance material more affordable

Plus a group of Internet mix feces stick

Defecate rubbish words on the site

This is how to prevent nausea NPC turnoff

In this fish oolong Parnassus Lane

Maybe I should have stepped down Chen Jinyong

Fangui my game

Street vendors also make a reality of these children

Just in front of the lighted

Where is our home

His wife asked loudly Ying

Tonight I have some little hostel rent

If tomorrow's business or sell poem so lonely

Your husband called me what should go

2005-11-16

Giood days

You ask a husband back

To my sorrows and joys, tears Gankaiwanduan

I could feel the hot towel

Zheng Chen wash away the blood and tears

Hot water body

My body heat to warm my heart

Q. between heaven and earth

Good wife why dash

Like an adult Ying wife

Happy to have you with at all because

Wanted dead

Worldly materialism

People selling merchandise I sell poetry

A few little text

But it is only the luxury of knowing each other

Concert of the

Moqiumoqiu

Exceedingly happy too

The wife and kids white picket fence

I asked the old lady feelings

Who needs only Astoria

2005-12-5

The lover online

Dear children

Speak the truth

I have repeatedly tried to run

However, I do not run off on your thoughts and love

Not run off your nostalgia and miss

I now finally understand

I love a person does not need too many reasons

Fall in love with a person may only hold in mind

Fall in love with a person may only common on inspiration

As you said

I was online only a few days

I confused my naked heart entrusted to a never met you

I had a suspicion, there have been questions

You are not really for me? Love me

I was not really in the mind can accommodate two women

I reflect, I asked

I was baffled

Why do I love you

You never met this woman dreaming

I have no answers and no solution to a problem

Some only is your Blanc and Caring

Can you tell me

Whether a person has a need for love

Whether you need one every day in total

I do not know, I do not know

I only know that my heart is still toward you

My love for you is still open

Only know how to love you is not easy

I love how hard it is helpless

Can not meet, can not hug

Trinidad kiss, love silent

Q. I heard God ah

Why teach people who love children so difficult

Cowboy really love, I would not help the situation

Weaver love, love in the soul heaven

Only by a cable v love

In the heart of the soul of our ideals draw a kingdom of love

2006-6-15

Love in the unkown place

miss you

You can not see me in the corner

Secretly thinking of you

love you

You do not feel in my heart

Bitterly in love with you

Maybe this time you

Are you joking with family

Maybe this time you

But lay your loved ones arms frisky

I like a wounded wolf in the wilderness Zhang Hao

Like a solitary male dog in the street choking

I howl

Howling sound can only be brought back sad

I cry

Ululation can hurt more

Love

Afraid to speak

miss you

Implicit dare

famous

Can not call

There are number

Dare pull

How much emotional love for you

Only knife to dig deep in my heart

2006-6-17

The love cannot be measured

I write you poems

Not use language to tell the story

I write you poems

It is from the depths of my soul for your true calling

You ask me how deep love you

I can not measure your foot intentions

You can measure your love ruler

Maybe the world really can not manufacture

Love your weight

Your realistic lover poet poetry only to feel

How deep is your love

Soul love for you to measure ruler

But that can not be labeled readings

For math teacher you

Only with love to sentiment

2006-6-18

The love from the poets

When you talk to ordinary people

You say just words

When you talk and poet

You must use your soul dialogue

Love someone

It can be like drinking water like dull

Fall in love with a passionate poet

You can not control your soul cry

Ordinary people to bring you

Maybe just instinctively feel marriage and sexuality

The poet brings you

It is the soul roam in paradise

The poet's soul poem agent

You can wash the dust of the world too much

Holy soul of a poet

You can cleanse your soul the dust oil

Fall in love with an ordinary person

You do not have happy

Feeling kind of fell in love with a poet

You'll have to groan in poetic

Even if only to hear your heart

                        2006-6-18

The sad evning

See people walking small mouth

Phase pull hand in hand

What a lovey scene

Wang Xiang Wei lover

Trouble was a sweet woman through the lottery male scene

I Zhichou passers audience

I do not know the East and West return

Sigh evening scene sunset West Ramp

He Shifei butterfly coming home

I do not know I do not know

Just two lines of Tears hung face

Fear persuade people

2006-6-19

Make the love to the end

How many times to

I want to tell you

But love in my heart

This world

Is marriage a piece of paper will be able to bundle our love

This is a false mask of morality

We should be so hypocritical pain alive

In this love can not communicate with the laity river

We only move forward

A love in the end

To persuade the world of the beloved children

We only dare Ganai

We can get spiritual holy love

We have no home

We can not even sex

But, my people children

I can not live without you in my heart

To our beautiful home together

We put down the mediocre man's face

We love love hearts

To our mind happy home tomorrow

Let us work together for the good of our souls

Realistic love for our

We will be in the end our love

Please shouted long live our love

If only wedding on the execution ground

We have to go forward

Love no regrets

For our supreme love

In this world

Nothing is not worth giving up

Please fire for us to really love beloved

Toward our soul strikes

                                            2006-6-20

The heartbreaking night

Not go to heaven

Could not make hell

Not love you

Hate you scared

Early see you

Night is not met Jun

Why Acacia

Why love

Entire heaven

Wrong to take the center line

But no one is born

Refuses even dead

My heart like fried

You do not hurt me

I pity Jun

Mandu grievances

Only timid Road

2006-6-20

The love at the end of the world

Read your

Only in my verse

miss you

I had to look up to the sky

love you

It is like waiting for the stars as unrealistic

Unexpected things always thinking

Impossible reality always look forward to

Videos One of the most delicious love yourselves

Let hunger passionate men and women to eat

To say

Speechless

Yuku

No Tears

I could not help feeling you

Love in the chest hard to open mouth

Say you

Then sentence me

This is a happy loving thing

Helpless far apart

Notwithstanding the worth of style

Also by the affectionate not tell

Love in the End of the World

Himself to the sky

Why should your club West home amorous

2006年6月22日

The coward's love

honestly

Dear children

I really want you to come with me

But you really come a

Maybe you and I will declare the disintegration of the family

You can not give you my feelings made me control

This is not the world's most anticipated is the love

Two affectionate men and women together

Can you guarantee it will not happen anything

You are not the

I am also not the

You are quite right

I am a coward

I was timid because I can not bear the weight of your love

Too heavy to disintegrate to the point where your family

You say, I have been able to own a private right of

I want your life all around me

I also think you can do this and that for me

I can see

I can smell the smell

You can stroking my chest

Listen to me an extraordinary love beating

However, you can dare

I dare to put a woman I love you to the career breaks

I'm watched her for me for Love

She watched as a realistic poet suffering hardship to do

I can not

I do not allow my love

I love her heart only for her sake

I really love her for her must be really good

Although, I really want to be with her

Really I want to live with her Enenaiai

However, I can do

I can not love her like ordinary people do

Reality and morality make us love it

I admit

I really love her

I love all her everything

But, in reality, allow me to love the person I want to love you

I also confess

I fear death

Behind me is the fear of death has not be informed of the difficulties

I am more afraid of death behind her is love

As Hello, my love

Please let me act as a coward now

The faint-hearted than I killed your strong poet

2006-6-22

Cannot love or hate you

I am leaving

But my heart is stayed

I am leaving

But my soul still wandering around you

Say go easy

Do not say difficult

My heart is hard to bear away your pain

I'm sick

Annoying sound in the absence of your days

I suffer

In the bitter sweet when you could not see my side

Maybe my extra people are asking for trouble

Thinking of you

Perhaps you and others are affectionate intimacy

I love you

But you're in the arms of others defected

Why should I bother

Why should I unrequited love

Fall in love with a man I do not know should not love

miss you

Want you and others common in pain

love you

Sad when you love and embracing others

You may not really want

You can not love

Hate you scared

Q. I heard my heart people children

You told me what to do

2006-6-24

The preface before the poem march

Dear children

Our poetry had marshalled

Our version of the kind already been printed

Our dishes have been burning success

The rest is just before the expedition of your words and explain

Maybe I can not

As tragic as the ancients said Zhuge Liang

"Inst" in spared no efforts in the death of subsequent words

I can not be in the ordinary happened

But he was loyal to the spirit of the Lord

The same can be reflected in my body

only

Poetry is not my home but my soul

Tell you, my loved ones child

I know: This is my personal journey

No spirits, no farewell ceremony

No flowers, no farewell exhort

Some just silent departure

I do not know how long the road ahead

I do not know how difficult the day after

But I love poem heart

Accompanied me singing all the way

Although I do not have your blessing

I can sincerely be your poetic heart

You like to be like flowers in full bloom

This is a great collection of poetry

I'm leaving

My beloved children

This is a poetic journey levy success

I know

I'm not good in front of the way to go

I know

I will be waiting for the difficult hardships

No horses, no money

Some only my writing talent

And I have a great love of poetry Poetic

I know

In today's social realities money

How hard is no money

Would like accomplishing a thing is how not easy

Even if you have a big writing talent

God can not have horses appear

This cruel world

Only by our tough heart

Only by our indomitable fighting spirit

I will ensure that my soul poem

Although, in addition to poetry, I have nothing

However, my work, my poetry

We will conquer the hearts of millions of people poem

This society, not the lack of money and most treacherous

But it comes from a sincere and honest conscience

No good work requires a certain publication

However, good works must let more people taste

Whether we use what way, method

But, I love people children

I tell you

I can not be buried

I can not help but know that good works

Not for money, nor for name

Not for interest, nor to the reputation

But, I love people children

We just let more people know

How beautiful is poetry

How poetry is sincere

Life as we expect it is poetry

As the poetic heart Fengyun sleepless

We have no reason not to give up our publicity work

In order to let more people taste more structured

We have thousands of miles verse

This is a helpless thing

It is also asking for trouble to do

I love people children

I do not need your blessing

I also do not need you greetings

I only need you to be my sincere

Regardless of the journey ahead

As long as you are sincere with

I will give us all the way to singing, all the way to the battle

Do not see me off

But, your heart must be accompanied with me

2006-6-29

The missing heart is still missing

People at night and think of

It's you

People eat sitting uneasy and uncertain

It's you

People desperate to go to the fire moths

It's you

Gu had people before but did not care for

It's you

Maybe one day

You will be in my backyard "fire"

You may miss your heart

Still reckless rush for you

What can I

Can control is maintained not want your mind

2006-6-30

The worrying heart's worry

You want in bed

Although sweet

But also worried

Sinister situation for your concern

love you

Though happiness was

Walks like angel-like in paradise

But also a dilemma

For Your

Which is not safe

Feel alarmed

Love your heart

At sixes and sevens

No peace for your well

I want to send text messages

Q. I heard you guys

Just can not

Afraid of my mind

Broken your safety

Left me

Only in your back

You secretly blessing

All right! My people children

2006-7-2

The lovers' in spirit

Daily companionship

Are your thoughts

If you just want to

Proof of

Just a touch of your love

If my heartache

That is deeply in love with you

People can not behave towards you

Japanese people think of you Night's Dream

People on their loved ones can not tell you is sympathy

The dilemma is that you people

People want to hide your loved one's life

All difficulties

All because you do not want to give up with a true love

Whether people accept it or not

I just want to say to you out loud

People I love

I will never accept you in the heart

My soul

All written for your sincere love

If the reality was so helpless in our lives really can not love each other

Perhaps one day we will go to extraordinary lengths

I went out to make a strange place we love

As long as we can hold love

That is worthy of our common destiny of love the Holy Land

For children who love to say

We spend a lifetime soul love

2006-7-8

The love like Coffee candy

Dear

In fact, true love

Just like a coffee sugar

When you did not go to it

You think

Common candy is the best

In fact, ordinary candy

Only freshwater marriage

When you do not taste the coffee sugar

Worrying about the kind of taste

You will not know the

You will misunderstand

The ordinary candy

As precious coffee sugar

And worse than their value

It is very great

Do not believe you went to the supermarket

Try and Buy

Taste test

2006年7月9日早

The best woman

I went shopping today

Look Woman

See a woman walking posture

The scene to see a woman walking

Speak the truth

Some woman is beautiful

Can be more beautiful beauties

You do not have in my mind is so beautiful

I appreciate

Called on the streets of the mobile landscape

I really can not taste

And you can be compared connotation

Can not understand

Can you touching the same quality

I scrutinized

I perceived only pedestrians hurry

not found

You my sweet nostalgia back

I realized

I just realized that the stranger's face loss

But I did not realize

Erotic kill you smiled feeling

2006-7-10

The hurt and love

There is a pain

It is not spoken

This pain

Is the pain from the depths of our spirit

There is a love

Also can not speak out

This love

From our soul is pure love

You can tell pain

That's not a big deal of pain

I can not say pain

That is what real heartache

This heartache

Can only be described as miserable

Love can tell

That's not much of a loved one

I can not say the unforgettable love

That is the true soul of love

This love

It can only be used to describe the supreme

2006-7-14

The best lover in life is my wife

Wife ah

No matter how wonderful the outside world

We did not settle down nest cute

No matter how fragrant flowers outside

Nor thriving home wife

Valentine beautiful

Just a short wine

Let me get drunk I do not know of Fangui

I do not know why just a few nights

But my good wife

But it is the best cup of fragrant Longjing

That refreshing tea

Will not let me groggy Zuoren

Drop intimate tea

Let me Mituzhifan husband

Turn over a new Zuoren

I admit

I was wrong, my good wife

The most wonderful thing good woman

Although your husband the poet bad guys

He can love your heart still lies

Although her husband as a poet I

Looking for a model of the original intention of love

To experience more "Love"

Make more love poems

But I was wrong, my good wife

Valentine heart is among the world's most unreliable

Even the best lover would not like my wife treated me like I love

No matter how much I eat bitterness out

Regardless of how much I driven to distraction on the outside

I can be a shabby poet

Let your wife also passionately devoted love to spoil

I was more difficult to see, and more ugly

But I still handsome wife in my heart

Her mind is still good husband handsome man

I also still is her favorite baby

Whether I have money or not

Regardless of wealth and rank me

My wife and I will still receiving

I will never betray

Also like a good dog like to follow in my side

Good wife

Not a cup of strong liquor

Good wife

Like clear soup pot pot

Taste beyond the boil

The more products the more flavor

No matter how old soup

Regardless of whether this soup unrecognizable

You can also taste good in my heart, in my poem

As my husband poet

Even if you are a wife yellow face

I will still love you

2006-7-22

The lonely wolf

I would like to say to you

I love people children

I forbid you to talk to random chaos Q

It is because I really care about you

Although I do not know

You in the end and who chat and who Q

Also whether it is male or female

The feet or legs of the chicken weasel

In short, I have to do is

I closed cages

Let all the dangers are gone

I carefully behind

It is with some care and intentions

I love people children

Others are content not to share

Whether at home or bee bee

It belongs to me flowers

I have to do a good job Huhuashizhe

Zhefan hard to pay

It will have a huge returns

Others generous

I do not appreciate

Love your heart

I have always been food alone pervert

My overbearing

Love is not allowed to tell justified

Common sense and conscience

Love your heart is concerned

Can not accommodate so-called ethical sermon

I only know

Love you can not go wrong

I think you can not go wrong

Love your heart is not unreasonable

Unreasonable heart will not love you

Both Beware thieves

It need not be afraid to make moral evil

Since love flower flower Pirates

It takes only open up for me! Flowers for my beauty

Others sarcastic agenda for what

We care

But I still love you

2006-7-23

The flying heart with love

Every morning

The first thing to get up

That greets you

Greeting message

Together with the love your heart

In flight

Button

I was struck in your heart the spirit of hand

Radio Cordless

Is the link you my love heart line

A press of a move

Are you worried about my thoughts

One word a word

Our language is the truth in love

Every move

We all really love the performance

Although separated by thousands of miles

But also soulmate

A hot one cold

It is also a foreign land with happiness and sorrow

Love does not hate late

Do not complain later met

Night Love

Only know how precious

Chi knowledge

He discovered the hard-won

Although the outside of love let us reason with unspeakable

But it was also frustrating fact that

Let us know

Sincere love how easy! How valuable can a song

Behind the unspeakable difficulties

We have a sincere love of a different kind of feeling

Road not suffering

Buried we met, love love surprises

I love it

I was in love with the people children

No matter how far we have

We must love hearts interlinked friend

We have a long and arduous journey regardless front

Our hands must be led, grip

Difficulties and obstacles

In love before we love

Without a trace

If we really love each other

Which cares high mountains, far from the road, something difficult, heart-breaking

Please according to our love atrium

Orientation toward where we are

Please people I love children

After our less prominent mobile phone

Let Mobile

Our love story passed incessantly

2006-7-26

The rhythm of love

Needless to say

Needless to say

As long as we have four-phase project, the two conditions dependent

Our eyes

We will be giving out endless love and our thoughts

All words

It seemed so pale and more

Our body language

It has emotional appeal language can not express

We entangled flesh

Showing endless lingering, Wife, love

He says the love you and miss you

Could only hand the baby boy or neonatal love

It will be so bland confession

as a

In the heart of someone who loves you

we

Like acting like that without telling Naiyouxiaosheng

We meet, meet, dependent

We hugged, with hold, connected

We need

Just enjoy each other in harmony in

We need to do

Just in a mood of joyous sense of rhythm Fangqing

Do a good role in our own sacred

Make their children and loved ones

Get supreme joy and happiness

We respect each other's wishes

We're more responsibility and reason

Let each other like herself for pleasure and enjoyment

We are not on earth to detect mineral treasure

We detected an earthly paradise where happiness

We are not looking for gold and silver

We are looking for the world of love and holy water Lequan

Open river landscape

Need ghost ax magic god-like skills

Looking for live holy water source

It requires skill and love at the same

Holy taste

Innocent and need love and common

Fun

It must be total commitment and intentions sentiment

my lover

The sweet taste we need to work together, cooperate with each other

We really need to appreciate the emotional phase will, dedication

Enjoy the passion we need to love the superb artistry of music played

2006-8-10

Talk about love

In case

Love

It is so readily available

Then

Love

Not more precious

in case

Love

It is without a lot of effort to obtain

Then

Love

Just mediocre release on behalf of the family group

in case

Love

Not what we would like to ask the dream

Then

Love

Not from the bottom of our hearts longing soul

People can live hard

You can not have pleasant dreams

People can live moderation

Keren can not have love hearts

But if a person give up his ideal

But if a person give up love hearts

Then it becomes meaningless alive and fun

All sorts of boring alive

This is no life force to live

This is not our hearts want wish

2006-8-12

The four word truth

Love together

Missed no love

Life geometry

Spring Night several times

Little love

Who scored a heart

True Feelings innocent

Moguan afar

Without further ado, cold-shouldered

Just love

Live life

It is like are left

The advance or retreat

Paradise Oliver

in a moment

Ask God laugh

Inviting a few people

Mo vain spring

Buried Love Bitterness

Wasted years

Old to shake sigh

Unfortunately, sad

                    2006-8-13

Without love, I would rather leave

Because dearly

Only heartache

Because tough love

Will cherish

Lu Yuan can not stop thinking

Tough love scare

Movies are not afraid of pure evil

Beloved to fear evil

Sorrow between lovers

Not that someone else's nonsense defamation

But rather the love between quitting

Let love in their eyes away

So happy floated around us

Self-sacrifice is the most worthless

Since only for combining family composition

No love nest as soon as possible in respect of child abandonment

If the people would not let us spend the day and night inviting

If you spend just to live and live

Then, spend the life is no fun in life

People spend it appears ignorant and Dasha

We want to be wonderful

We need to live with love there music taste

If only reluctantly let us spend time guarding phase

Emigrated is our best choice

And people who love to eat light point

And no love stronger than people who live in high-rise buildings

2006-8-14

The woman's heart and love

You can plain

You can not high not low

Your body also like a general

but

You have to let your loved one's heart happy

because

People there

The most happiness and joy are not material and money

But feel the heart and soul of

You do not have money

You can not have a car and a house

You can no longer high current income

but

You have to make your loved one feel like you have something to look forward

because

People there

At present, life is not equal to the bad state after bad

Environment will change

As long as shrewd and hard work pay

The future will change tomorrow

You can not have a good mom and dad

You can not help the Master

You can now have nothing further

Can you

You have to let people think you love is a rare good man

Let her think

You are worthy of her lifelong companion entrusted

Let her feel

She'll tell you the joy and happiness

She confirmed

You're her future and longing

Because: smart woman

It will not matter as the first choice

Talent is fundamental

Heart is the key

Love is also on this basis

Any money and material linked to love

It is a misunderstanding of the innocent

Love for slander

As the basis for binding

The combination of both substances

Marriage is only required for the combined

The combination of only two sexes combined

And desires of human instinct

True love never said humanity

Only an idiot would recognition

2006-8-27

I am saying goodbye to you

No message

No greetings

Perhaps this is the reason we have forgotten each other

Alienate and silence

Avoidance and unfamiliar

Perhaps implying

We are mutually forgotten

Fade out and leave

Maybe you really are my best choice

A stupid man

I do not know unfamiliar shown after

Only a fool dementia inconsiderate

No longer continue to have a strong emotional love story

Perhaps finish at the curtain call in relation to this

Alone singing love drama

Is sad clown and acting

To love and be loved

To voluntarily by both parties want to

Any party to insist on love

All heart unwilling, reluctant robber love

Any substance as the temptation of love and money

Not so much from their own inner feelings in love

As it is in the possession of or misappropriate the strongman "love"

The substance of love is from the soul, though not the true love

However, it is a lot of people what they need to material type so-called "love."

I was loved and I loved the people

I would like to say goodbye and thank you in this

This is me, you also

After the farewell loved and been loved said

I would like to give up my feelings for you

However, it does not mean that we must reject once had loved

I would like to return to my emotional journey

This is not the same as you would have to complain of feeling I've ever had

I know you are more difficult to understand your decision

Perhaps we do not speak of their departure is our best choice

Because: you do not want to hurt me

Like I do not want to hurt like you

Silence silence is the best way of parting

As reasonable people on

Maybe we really have to re-home for

That some love, love should not have

Some of this situation, the situation should not have

These must go to clean up the source

For the home is

The most important thing is to live today and tomorrow live

2006-9-3

Complain about husband

Blame a husband

Do you really know what's good

Your date night Internet access

Japan also has Q Q Night

Q I do not know why they are reluctant to leave too

Q wife was heartbroken and helpless and cool

Q wife was not home like home wife well, unlike public

Bad bad one thousand Wan

Bad thing is the bane of this network cable

One thousand Wan complain complain

He spoke against computer QQQ husband gone I Heart

You may not want to eat

Sleepy night

Only keep a computer

Just you, you love me I chat on the web of addiction to

FIG merely Xu Xu Xu Qing phoney online to Xinmi

Others say a shameless love senile

Wife behind the female side

Bed table husband's father

A family room is also old is not serious

Has a wife and daughter would like to have Gesha

I still love you online hypocritically

But I do not know how many laughs bad breath how much saliva

Presbyopia you to send nerve

You stole Yeshi not steal this at home

Within ten feet of you or my husband

Since ancient times, good prevails over evil

We have the ability to call your online lover and I singled out

You say your head sore foot discharging downright bad

You smuggle her husband's emotional love smuggling

You Chuaizhuo bowl was thinking pot

You no small ambition deserted you

You halfway decent work you want to find another new love new love

You say you really epilepsy epilepsy

If you are stupid you silly

Sincerely for hello is not yet home Huanglian Po

If you do something unexpected should happen

Interpreting your heart for you to worry about your wife's not me

If someone else's good wife

That is because your woman really useless

If you can answer online Valentine Love

You jackass will hold computer to overnight

You knock on the keyboard will be able to eat

You have the ability to eat tonight my aging mother do the cooking

A wife does not love you mess madness

I also love those that love

Dog mouth spit you only ivory

If you believe the words sister network

Sows can climb trees to sleep

You do not believe this silly you Q

Are QQ sister network with you this wood duck sleep

You can also talk to tease

Online Valentine's letter can not be

As for poetry to you for

If you Nongjiachengzhen I'll cut you always lifeblood

Saying that when I marry you

Not a house not for money

Not height not appearance

Only for you this poor boy Fengyun heart poems

Unable to rise

Live Mansion

Not greedy rich

Officials and businessmen do not plan

I just want your kid to be good in the future

Sylvia Woods heart poetry

All words to love all

I loved the small day you Huan

Evening worthwhile worthwhile spring

Say a husband you

Wrong to change, not ever study

Since you want to change the network situation

You do not mess dubious to Q

If you do not say a decent word

My wife to pull your cable seal your computer

See you and talk about what

Hello had a dog with me

I cook for you for your laundry

Wholeheartedly serve you

Housekeeping for you as you daughter fertility

You only live like a pet pet tortoise

Let your music to make you worry

I thought to let you make your heart sick

2006-9-4

We cannot compete with time

Whether you glad Hao

No matter no matter whether you worry

Time and things will slowly torture your mood

Make you cry nor laugh nor to

Things to be so helpless that you

You do not have to accept the accepted

The reality is this torture people

How are you and Yuna reality

Time will make you forget the pain

Time also makes you old heart slowly

Only the mind is numb

The bloodshed and sorrow not only heart

Tears would have let the wind dried

Numbness of the face buried a lot of frustration

Shouting and laughing reality can not do nothing

Happy things are always quickly on the past

We can escape only with expressionless endure

Silence will become our ultimate resistance selection

Because: We are not rivals of time

There are many things are not what we think by the wish

2006-9-14

The arts of football

When a player the ball hit the door

The ball is fired into more than

But fame and money

Happy to say

In fact, it is not just the ball into

Or a terrific game

The real excitement came in the excitement or integrated

Individual achievement is to be divided is future

So why should not coach

The club and do business

It is self-evident

Well fans

Perhaps it is not really a gambler Dasha

Players in the field just monkey

If poor performance which monkeys

Next is nothing to say the

To know this is not a ball and ball

Nor is it to enjoy music

You represent the interests of a whole

Which door stuff never let the overall interests of the more inviting

2006-9-18

The good wife does not manage husband

Good wife

Do not discipline her husband

Her behavior and emotions

Naturally ambitious probation prodigal husband

to be frank

I am a man Huahuachangzai

If not met all aspects of a woman to my satisfaction

I really difficult tied down quite contented Fengyun ambitions

The temptation too much outside

If your wife is not a good woman

Like me ungrateful shit poet husband

Indeed is a center of the old wolf

The ancients said: people do not romantic only for the poor

I can only love and romantic poetry

And all I've ever had with a woman

No one is not to take to coax soul and poetry

I admit

I am not a good man

I'm not a good husband

I use my dog feces Xu Qing and I like poems captured your heart

I'm a bad person and describe the Inner Voices in your heart this clean sheet

For me

I love you really like Mice Love Rice

Really speaking

Since we met each other since

You've been really treated me love me

Restless only hardened my Fengyun bad heart

You just bent toward my blooming love makes me feel inferior

Clean your heart so I have nothing to say

Although, I have to nitpick looking for an excuse

I still nothing

In front of you such a good woman a good wife

I hypocrisy

When is your body is not afraid of shadow oblique opponent

I addition to repentant

A love of the truth to you outside

What better be you

2006-9-19

Successful businessman

Good Businessman

Not only will make money machine

Good Businessman

No matter how you succeed in business

If you're after a successful career

Do not make charitable

Quit in favor of the people and the nation useful things

So, your success

We can only prove

You're just a money-making machine

No matter how much your net worth

You most admire are only money you have and worship

remember

As a truly successful businessman

Not just big money will do business people

You need to have more than the average person more compassionate and responsible

Fu bigger role in your body is to return to the community

Not a return to the community

A people without the benefit of a Fang Limin

One pair of their own country and nation indifference businessman

No matter how your business empire mostly strong

They are not worthy of praise

In front of the nation and society

Your heart can only prove: Money, Money

After you successfully

Only a return to the community treat people

You will not forget this kind-hearted look

Because: The ultimate purpose of business success

Not just let you have more money and businesses

But to give you a greater return back to society your own people

This is a successful businessman and the owner's responsibility conscience

2006-9-23

Move away from Guangzhou

Say good Guangzhou

As my foreign visitors

During this brief few days

I feel

I admit

Guangzhou than the north,

It can be big enough does not mean

I have to admit

Building and green Guangzhou and better looking than the north,

As humanities community

Affection and harmony is more important than appearance

Perhaps, Guangzhou Yangcheng people will say that I am ignorant

As a stranger to Guangzhou a few days

Perhaps, really not qualified to make irresponsible remarks in Guangzhou

It can be used as an outsider I

I have to say my heart's experience and feelings

Speak the truth

I used to envy the big cities

That: in the big city life must be better than living in a small city

But when I came to Guangzhou

I appreciate the real

Red wine, green living

It was just the rich life

In big cities

As people of civilians

It must be put off as a slave to money

In the big city life of ordinary people

Many of the original nature so long ago the big cities suffering beyond recognition

Ordinary people living in Guangzhou

Although blocks of high-rise buildings that look good and beautiful

Layers can house but it is not written the word prison cell semicolon

Such is the heart cells

Some people might also suffer the same as house slaves send away

Say travel

The billowing dust exhaust

Indeed suffocating uncomfortable

When the traffic jam scene

Really daunting

Because there is not much money

At present, many people in Guangzhou, the car is also too poor to feed the affordable

That fight is not to think about things

Unless there is an emergency or when filling bulk fight

This play taxi

Most of foreign visitors is dedicated slaughter work

For not much money for civilians

The fight is not really the preferred

Since I do not play

That would have blackmailed tough

Fast on the road as a rat

Jiju would like sardines as flexible

You get the same treatment as the surrounding people like Fangzei

Because you are in the bus environment

Many people are unfamiliar foreign

The broadcast bus seated morality

It seems to be howling at the moon in the irony Huaer

Because: sitting or standing here most indifferent living thing rather than the soul

Do not believe, you see their faces apathetic

Indifferent expression suggested that

People here incorrigible

Look street security patrol

Handheld Tiecha barbed embattled scene

Indicate where security is not optimistic

Here is the proof everyone

The massacre is everyone's inner soul

Shown here are human hearts unpredictable

to be frank

Guangzhou is too big, too chaotic, too many outsiders

Guangzhou had to treat people

If you let my wife and children live in such a situation

I am one hundred unwilling

Our town is not big though

Needed to be enough in our lives

No money to buy a car

Riding a motorcycle everywhere channeling

When the mood

And his wife Ingrid on sprucing up our piece of land dishes

Live this half farming half read how good life

For my heart souls

Guangzhou Yangcheng Hopefully goodbye forever

2006-10-4

Please call home

I was getting impatient waiting for you

I was waiting for you, etc. Interpreting

But you still did not come back

I'm anxious home

As night falls early

You ought to go home yet to come

Early bright street lights outside

Heavy traffic yet to see your shadow on a motorbike

Lighted the lit my anxiety, worry

I was re-dial telephone in

Can your "PHS" or in spirit and not pass

This is really disappointing telecom heart unhappy people hate

You can not solve the technical, do not deceive money harm Interpreting

To know the customer's connection is not there just call Interpreting

To say the truth to your wife Huaer

This home not lack your wife ultimately my husband

I assume your body is not only the obligations and responsibilities

And we open the door to the old love mind and soul

We have no reason to refuse to build a house, have for love

This home is a sound that you need me

So, your wife back late

In relation to the family call

So as not to worry about your family too

2007-9-1

The slave of real estate

I do not envy is the main room

In this small county

In fact, the developers and banks are the real Zhuer

In order to have a small home to settle down

Afraid developer of the "intimidation"

If we do not buy a house mortgage loans

We will no tiny bit of land in the city

Midnight cry wife could not bear to look poor

That want to have a small family of strong desires

I can not help but cross under a pauper perseverance

To the wife and children a stable JINWOZI

A part of our own warm home

Shattering even have to buy the house

No house wife can not stand the torture of grievances

Listen to the real estate agency beautiful vision Temptation

Faith bank's generosity and generosity

that's it

A poor little husband finally the blue sky for the family

A shrewd man perplexed final on someone else's "pirate ship"

Builders for the rest of his life and contribution to the bank the day has finally arrived

Living beyond, the more their brains way of life has begun

It awaits us will be a difficult city house slaves life.

2008-11-29

The Sun in the heart

When things did not develop according to our thought

When we pay all the efforts are in vain

Time and patience when we can no longer tolerate the situation when

We say what man can conquer nature of faith

That really is nonsense to say presumptuous fool

A borrower poet Li Bai I'm Born with speech

People are ignorant of self-comforting words

Hopeless and helpless self-deception masturbation mentality at play

Hundred no one was a scholar

On the set of the ancients we are really not against posterity

At least that is our people who write poetry like this

Things are beneath contempt, only high school of Don fallacy lies

Economic wealth has long been overthrown was erased

People and society is looking forward to riches and economic development

So please do not say with poetry

Poetry now really die

Today's society is not poetry society

Really, do not say others say you are a poet

People will laugh at you behind Yanzui mad

Even if you stop what poetry forums, websites

There just self-righteous who mixed poetry world

Shit every day painting chaos days

Or attack this or that evil

So I do not know pandemonium

Let people think all of them are poets, poetry everyone

But all of them are not a poet, everyone just scribble

In fact, the real treat Poetic

Only in our hearts poetry

Only in our hearts we have the pure land of poetry

Where will fit in this clean Poet

We seek not only is the poetic heart to accommodate real Poet

Impetuous social and materialistic people is no longer a paradise of poetry

Only poetry is our people own mind really is poetry in mind the sun

2008-12-8

The car models

See you handsome appearance of eye candy

The pure color without stunning body

It will also allow the devil back to health taste

You beautiful skin and a devil figure

It is for people with a woman's shame

Being a woman is really vastly different

No matter what kind of attitude you put modeling

All for our consumers Erotic, kill, seize money

You also want to put your beautiful temperament

Bring out your endorsement of the brand car really is different

You let a man spit extend three feet is not only natural beauty

So that men can not help but want to have you there and beauty Dream Car

Car makers is bad water We thought the man's desire

Let us feast for the eyes behind it is high-value cars worth

Cunning car commercial you unique native feminine

Beauty in our heart we bitterly Henzai consumers knife

Regardless of whether the knife with blood dripping a lot of money

All this pay

We all want to buy a car can be as perfect as you

Although we knew the car dealer in Jiehuaxianfo tippler Italian

But also how car makers in daring to set off the green leaves from gild

With your cute temperament capture our gluttonous selfishness

With your beautiful landscape of our hanging high appetite of consumers

The real intent is like a hook Millionaires like us as pig slaughter

We are not afraid to say the car the kids

We do not reject the beautiful and pure

We also do not refuse sexy and Quality

Although we every man has the heart of beauty

However, we will resist the temptation and greed

We will reject carnal lust

We will reject and naive delusions

Although, this is self-comforting helpless confession

You can clearly understand our hearts

Multi-car pretty baby can only be deemed to enjoy the landscape like

like! But we can not really love each other and have

Because: Your vision is too high, too big dream

Husband hit your mind, the wealthy are too many

We civilians it is not his opponent

Beautiful baby car can not enjoy our bread and water

Can watch

I love you neither realistic nor practical

Perhaps the presence of your baby's car just to demand a role Bale

In the eyes of your car's only eye-catching bait tool

2008-12-18

The world of dream

I can not eat now

Also can not wear

I can not live again

I really want to live the way as I do

I really can worry regarding the peace of mind to do what I do the things you like

difficult

This is prohibitively difficult

We are a middle age man who told

Why did we have under the old and the young

We are also inviting aspire good wife

Householder must not decide who must decide

Home of the main ridge beam does not pick who picked task task

Tianzhu not worry about the top home home home home home who worry

To our lovely little home

We must make a man willing involuntarily cattle

Think of the days when single

Really carefree

No family out of danger

When young childlike nostalgia

Just not hungry, any time I want to play with the East and West

Geometric young

Ignorance from the music

Only way is pregnant with married love, color security responsibilities in music

Silent smile

Tastes just buried my heart knowing

Responsibility than days

How can thoughts

How emotion

The hardships of life

The sinister heart

We can not mediocre men about

Dreams can

Life must still be

Only in an ideal world we sleep occurs

Qingxin want refined writing

Only when wake up is Qinglei

Let us also somewhat sane

Life must continue to take steps

Tomorrow the sun is still Dongsheng man warned us: Responsibilities must bear

In order to support their families

Sishibuhuo also a man rushing toil leather own life

For the family to live incumbent

Dream world can only hope to show in our soul of a poet

The reality of life only relentless torment numb conscience

2009-1-10

About these experts and professors

On CCTV military program

Look military experts and professors to explain aircraft, tanks, nuclear knowledge for boats

It is like a master known as a sermon proficient homemade

Let us smattering of military fans

We had to prostrate to convince the military masters very knowledgeable

Experts and professors of the military is really nothing to understand, omniscient

They look at the forecast CCTV military program of military fighting

Army fans ignorant of us have deeply felt

But afterwards he stopped short laugh

Blame our initial ignorance by confusing too

Commander in Chief also fortunate countries Fortunately, not these experts and professors

Otherwise, a war occurred but

As for these experts and professors as a military command

It makes no subjugation genocide battered country

These military experts, professors

Military combat and weapons secrets on

Really better than the play also funny clown

To know military secrets is the lifeblood of the country to the door

So it goes on TV to talk about the big secret, said vent

Trying to fool us in the majority of TV viewers rhetoric is compromised as a traitor traitorous

If the NSA is not allowed to seek them squatting behind bars

If the real weapons manufacturing experts ridiculed all Yanzui

It would prove

These so-called military experts and professors in nonsense

In deceived and fooled the majority of military fans

CCTV military program might really need someone to perform the role as a self-righteous ignorance

And all just to make the program and the program fills

2009-1-28

The poet shouldn't have a marriage and family

Since we like the Broncos as a free letting their emotions

We have no ability to control whether our love loyal

Temperaments and always with poetry drift

We will not be holding enduring affection

When God gives us is a passionate kind of bohemian

We would not be a competent husband and wife

We also will not be an honest partner

Why did we have a sleepless Poetic

Why did we have is an impure heart and soul and Wainian

Why did we have six more dirty mind dreams

Splenetic not only our emotions passion

More disappointing is that we have someone with a heart that can not be some poems

We use poetry to beautify what we do,

We also used the poem already ugly dress up our heart and soul

We decorate our crown poetry dirty shameless show role

We also shouted hurray for our actions

I do not know shame to sing the praises of low quality

We are human beings

Is a poet can not be compared with ordinary

Nothing is done a general guideline poet lover

We can not close our live poetry poem heart

We also can not control our impetuous poetry

We can not be done that I could love a lover's wish

We will not afford the responsibility of ordinary ordinary husband

Although we human parent Mrs.

We do not necessarily comply with common sense vulgar Regulation

When we encounter inviting people and things

We have to show a random verse poetry without taboo

Poetry to ecstasy

Love to concentrated at

We also really false, false is also true reality into live action role

We can no longer grasp the truth of love angles and objects

Mistakes will be inevitable

Bad behavior will show the true nature of our original poet

We are a poet

And we have our own love and the reality of home

We can not afford ordinary family responsibilities

We can not reject his wife's rebuke and blame

We compare the ability of ordinary people competent

We will have to bow to silent nagging wife by telling

A poet who told us

And will not do is a get word poetry poet

Perhaps the real poet is a marriage and family should not have

Because: We are living in the world of poetry who dissent

We can not make the world of poetry into the real life of the perfect man

Real poet maybe does not apply to any competent to make a real husband and parents

The poet will fit in between heaven and earth sing poetry fugue

2009-1-30

Hard to get a true female friend

Wife readily available

Hard to find the roots

Yong congregation are snobbish world

Red Dust

None of intimate

No confidant

Cross pen laughing

Sigh world confidante rare earth

Goodly

His talents and ambition who tell

Heaven alone poetry

No list of Comrade

Dongfeng will not sigh and Shuro

Ming Bao talented, not in perfect

2009-2-5

The real meaning of life

Life is not because you are having a harder and sympathize with you

Life is not because you live frugally and appreciation to you

In fact, life more because you do not blame you a nice luxury

Praise and appreciation of life would give birth to only those people who will live and

Life has always been a hodgepodge of music

Different people have different ideas of taste

Maybe you feel the taste of the bitterness of the bitter life

Others may experience of life is sweet syrup

This I tell you wrong, you are my non-controversy already ridiculous ignorance

Who is subjective meaning of life just off the shallow Solutions

Life itself is not to deny the affirmative and that right and wrong

In fact, the original meaning of life is vary

Way of life may be different as possible

As long as you fit lifestyle

Then you should enjoy life

Tastes good feel for life

As long as you remember and understand

Life itself is not too hard on you or favor

You have no ability to fight or not to adapt to life itself

In fact, as life and life is fair

It is not because of some people rich, more money to let their nice smooth sailing

Because some people will not let it sit back and relax high position

Life and life as something to be lost

Will naturally belongs to you belongs to you

Not belong to you must not insist on

Unfair just human society and the human self

Request is too demanding and misconceptions about life and the violation

If you are unhappy and disappointed because to live to complain

If you cause to live rich and happy cheers

That is not where the life of the request

In fact, life itself is everyone has his own living law

Ask of life is contentment, self taste the joys

Students can live in respect glad to meet, from the music

At least compared to those who are seriously ill or unfortunate for

How lucky can be safe and happy, and healthy living

Life is already short

We live in the world the day is not long slow

Life is proud to be thoroughly enjoyed themselves

This is what is at fault

Can not enjoy sharing, music can not be happy that this is not a good idea

Frail heart is weak you will know regretted pure ignorance

So, when conditions

How can we must be happy but not happy the reason

We must fight back or forced to lead a hard life is not the intention of living

What is wrong comes naturally to live the way

Interpretation of life is to know that we both have to know how to live green

2009-2-12

Only the emotional women have the true love

If you want to dominate women

Then you let her be your queen

If you want to get rid of a woman

Then you let her sad despair

A woman's heart is the emotional heart

A woman's heart is vanity heart

For the emotional woman

Nothing you let her make you a happier God

Women want to feel the most is that you most care about her feelings

Let her indulge in your love is the best panacea

Mystery and confusion in your tender devotion to her dream is to get you the best way

She is her obedience obey your best strategy

Give in it shall be thoroughly

For the emotional type of woman

You love her pay is far smaller than she loves you pay more

Emotional woman rope shall be implicated with emotion as

Let a woman dancing with you then have a feeling that you love best guarantee

As a spiritual woman emotion

Live in the emotion is more important than living in reality

As her lover

You not only want to feel her feelings are thinking

You need more control and guide the good woman's inner feelings

Grasp the soul of a woman's heart

This was more than eager to love money and material pain

Only materialism heart strong woman

In order to break this door by emotion

Ask for money with a strong woman

Emotion will be deemed to fart stink

For the women of money worship

Money is the sincere desires of their eyes

Love in their eyes are just as superfluous as Tuoku fart

These types and a woman falling in love is like 狸猫换太子 like sad

Emotional love in their hearts to the market to buy or sell it as easily as

Only emotional woman will have a true love

Shown any love

Not from want in inner feelings of love are false

Such hypocritical love do not have this matter

Good face and body

Seductive and good will on behalf of food color

But not necessarily representative of a beautiful love and future

Marriage requires money as a support operation

Love is only sincere emotion pay each other the truth

Regardless of whether this really loved for a long time

Regardless of their ability to withstand torture marriage and money

However, this kind of emotional love

But it is sincere, the heart of love

Even if its short

But also our lives the most beautiful and pure love lies

In addition, other loved ones are obviously hypocritical! Not worth talking about

2009-2-18

The last stage of life

Song from the song down

People dancing people scattered

No matter what changes dances

The same is still the heart of the dance floor rejuvenate the elderly

Fatigue lifetime of bitterness thing of the past

Old music fun to be confirmed in the aunt, uncle Yang overflow their smiling faces

Old people also eventually be able to release red heart in dance in old age

How Mock aged waist stiff swing

Late in life to take the final steps

Ye laugh, boast worth mentioning

The old ways of the world from the music

The world is crazy dance from

Sit on the sidelines

Singing a song

How much bitterness of joy is in the music dance

Fail, if I succeed

Finally ordained gains and losses

Mo on the white and black

How he managed unpredictable morals

Wu forget how many vicissitudes

Then dance on a night when the song from the music

Tomorrow's stage who knows if there's cheerful white-haired dancer

Noh and music, and singing songs too

When the dance of its own finish

Night life drunk worthwhile song

Dancers from the music only

Old people had to worry about Mo

In stage

As much as possible with the music and dance

Elderly people at

Only dance and eventually resigned

Today, dance is perhaps tomorrow Elegy

Now dance is perhaps the end of the last traces of life character asks

Elderly people in public places is perhaps the last paradise perfect life's journey

Please lot of understanding and tolerance in most good public space occupied by mostly elderly

The final curtain call of life only in terms of dancers dances

2009-2-21

Readers cannot understand poets

Poetry has always been good

Beauty is not just some product poet's heart

Poetry is not vicious

Splenetic often just ignorant people who do evil Poetry

Not because of some "Poet" decadent indiscriminate attacks on the quality of poetry

Do not work is because some dog feces put all the poems as evil

You do not like some of the poet may not be representative of all poets

You like some of the "poet" Maybe not on behalf of his "poem" is superior

Poetry ugly, mediocre poetry and extraordinary because it is not your personal preferences veto

In fact, in real life

Behaved so-called "good" as the poet is often not good poems to

Because: Spirituality sentiment poetry often just "lucky" to have the mind of a poet

Normal state of mind like that it is impossible to make absolutely beautiful poem

When you ask the poet's heart seems like you when

You're asking a poet, like you mediocre and clumsy

Vulgar vulgar heart will experience things

Elegant poetry only high-quality heart and soul Experience

Brilliant poems should also be people who can taste a little literary talent

Yong congregation need to read only the popular vulgar stuff

Perhaps this statement will make some people feel dissatisfied

To know is not well-off life on behalf of its noble spirit soul happy

Poet ugly character is not representative of the quality of its poems

In fact, the poem itself only recognized the merits of the essence of poetry

Our products enjoy good poetry requires only poems

As for the poetry of life and I acted

We, as readers really to criticize and preaching

Because: We do not understand what the author was feeling creative

We also do not know the author's living environment

We do not necessarily have more time author writing talent

Therefore, we have no right to ask authors like us live and think

We also have no right to veto the poet more actions, thoughts

We just need to taste good poetry itself

We also need to appreciate the poetry of real Smirnov

As poetry is superior Libertine how "bad" in order to make it without sophisticated

Of course, there is another matter pseudo-poet

2009-3-5

To thoese city administrators in China

I'm afraid you

However, even though I was really afraid of you

However, I have to say to you

I know you can

Able to free the oppressed only for meals rushing toil peddlers

Because: they are weak urban poor groups

Because: They are chaotic pendulum chaos sell, do not abide by the rules of the inferior "trouble-making"

Because: they are doing is impaired in the "civilized" cities "uncivil" behavior

But also because: They do not obey your uncle discipline and expulsion

Even if it is to maintain a livelihood of small business have to look at the color of your uncle

I know you cow

Cattle are free to take the spoil grab something small traders and farmers

Even poor old honest farmers were not spared vegetables

Because: they sell the place is really beautiful and elegant Obstacle

Because: They bragging, I do not know who is the uncle of the city bullies

Because: they do not understand morals, I do not know who owns the geographical scope of jurisdiction

But also because: they are persecuted for no one to seek justice for their grievances little people

What civilized law enforcement? Serving the people

Their small business, hawkers, farmers do not understand guys

What hearing? What single buckle open procedures

This is simply unnecessary trouble superfluous things

Treat small business, hawkers, farmers guys just fist

How can grab

How can took

How can ruin

How can broad daylight

How can self-dealing

How dared argue hit you

We have the ability to tell my uncle chased

The city did not have the small traders and farmers guy almost deprived

Cry? Tears? Who pity you

You can not stretch to injustice

Here's axiom does not belong to you

You can not have in vain to call

The right to speak here also do not belong to you

Want to know: regulations, rules are not set by you

Chased my uncle took a feather when the authority arrow can

Besides a truth

City should not belong to your small business, hawkers, farmers guy geographical scope

How do you survive to support their families do not shut my uncle chased

Small business, hawkers, farmers guy but do not know the rules of morals

Easy to be a gentleman, no good Inferiority

Bullied poor and weak, the strong do not commit

Urban wisdom

Good heart which will not be chased

Evil people will not need humanity

Royal Highness is the fist

Axiom is overbearing

Urban actions is the "enforcement" People

I serve! I serve! I serve! I serve you some fucking uncle chased

I just want to say

Grab what you can not grab poetry

Because: poetry scold your inner soul

You go grab my poems, but did not take away my

You go grab Cantos text but can not take away my soul writing poetry

You have to destroy the fruits but can not destroy the beauty of poetry goodness

You have to go get it take away my belongings Goods Poetic inspiration

I know

I'm not against you chased in the city

But, I also know

My poem heart will condemn you in the poem is the root of all evil

Unless you let conscience eating Tengu

Items not rush to take the spoil of beauty in the world

Oppress the weak will be the story of the evil Joker

Poverty is not a shame

Strong is not good

Do not lose heart from the good

Only ugly evil spirit

The poet God sending you some advice chased

Human heart only for repair and charity Jide

Life Mo selfish self-interest have heart

To do good life, do not bully Gouzhangrenshi

2009-3-11

Live

I hope alive

Live is happy

Live is life is good

Is alive means that the future of tomorrow

To live is to their lives and their families the best reward

Regardless of whether live suffering hardships

You can live a thousand times better than dead

Poverty is not even alive sorrow is despair can not survive

There is life there is hope, there is life there is the future

For the purposes of the dead alive and that it was really nothing

So, better than anything else alive

Even if it is also sad to live longer than the dead strong

Alive not only their respect for life is responsible

Alive is responsible for their own family and their mission

Alive not just your own personal things

Alive and well-being related to the entire family whether sound

For families alive

Alive is really precious happiness

For people who are alive

At any time do not easily give up their lives

Because: you have no right to treat life rash

Just reckless abandon alive

This is a violation of life

This is also the family and their irresponsible stupidity of

Ignorant people who have no reason and excuse to stifle the presence of God gives you life

Death is definitely not the best choice

In peacetime years

Bring only death of their loved ones is a long psychological grief and pain

Can pain relief may only be selfish you personally

When we lose our loved ones

Living can only be the last moments of their loved ones back in our minds Movies

Alive for the family to leave will be immortalized in terms of lack of bereavement

For students who are alive

Alive becomes more valuable, cherished self-love

2009-3-18

How to get a good wife

Although beautiful love

Marriage is a bumpy winding rugged mountain road

Despite the perfect lover

That's because pre-marital forget or ignore its shortcomings created

Even useless wife

But also because Xiangxie live day bears cause wasted years

Since the choice of her as a wife

Life must be accompanied with her bald, sharing a bed with the old days

Now that she recognized as the final journey of life partner

Must be dedicated to the teachings of his wife he thought the perfect emotional world

Good Mind has a natural course of the ingredients into the nature

But good wife that her husband taught well and acquired properly guide

If you thought, as her husband was happy smug

So, tuning guide wife heart with the desire of the mind training programs must be launched

Beautiful woman's natural need to add chicken soup pot married husband teach considered perfect

Even the appearance of a good woman born to create pleasing

Good wife was acquired by the "crooked" only husband tuning out personally taste

Man thought too happy liking

Man must be wondering training wife to her husband as the most important heart love Cardiff

The first is to let his wife know

I love my husband more understanding in relation to her husband's wishes ambition

My husband likes to make her husband happy is to be happy happy place

This kind of sophistry favorable husband must instill brainwashing many times to be effective

Psychological counseling sessions wife must be on foot Shanghao Mozhun

I thought of my wife wished we must grasp guide appropriate

Only in this way, we will all wishes come true for men

Only in this way, we make her husband the day before the arrival of the sweet

Believe it! The world thought about the good old days of the husband who has a wife

Good Wife is really the soul by tuning out

Among the world you have never had a most agreeable wife

Good wife by her husband is often out of hand tuning

I thought enjoyable day

I wanted to make her husband happy

That good tune yourself for your good wife

The world has never been a wife is to obey her husband in every possible way

Only hard work is paying teachings wife thought her husband would be the most understand love

Of course, I said good refers to her husband's genuinely good

The "good" of course, including your good dreams

Husband to be "true meaning" of his wife taught more truth will become famous natural deep affection

Repeatedly brainwashing preaching good wife to her husband also will be allowed Accreditation is granted

Husband roses every day will lead a happy life

Do not believe you to try

2009-3-28

To HanHan: be nice

I think this sound

Patient may not equal to a sign of weakness

I again online

On the Internet to see again and again in your whole evil attack Parnassus

My patience your heart again and again by your ignorance can not bear irritated by it

Although everyone knows that today's poetry is poetry clutter fish

Some poems are mixed and hang sheep head pseudo-poet in poetry circles spoof, random defecate garbage words

You really should not be ignorant of the whole Parnassus ruined shelling all poets

A stick and knocked the whole practice of people on the boat really ignorant, shallow

Scholars light as it should

Wounding pain if you do not want to say this

You can also self-righteous behavior ignorance really is people have to say

What you see is not inferior poet on behalf of all poets

You have to watch the free tourist strip show is not on behalf of real poetry by

As you taste the pie is even more true of the whole world will not be the best to eat pie

These people are not real poet

These people just spoof their own

Even if it's linked to what the official called Sheepshead national poet

It would never work on the recognition of their outstanding and outstanding writing on

I cried for you in this Han

They are not really a poem, poets

They are just in their own "poetry" in masturbation acted in ignorance not only of the people

People recognized the quality of work rather than just false title

Readers loved poetry is just poetry itself was in no way writing is laced with gold mask

The same is true you Han

Whether you "triple gate" or Nine lock worth mentioning

The book is not selling you on behalf of Han have writing talent

This may only show your bookseller touted clever marketing successfully implemented

Money will not only show you are engaged in fiction genre is very popular

Or booksellers and fans for all your support special attention

Nor can a lucky man cursed it does not exist another poet

Touted hype, the use of which is evident to see things

You really think their works are selling well is to have writing talent

You really think he is the elite? Insufferably arrogant

Other modern poets are damned poor

Han big money writing fiction you live in relation to

This is too shallow and ignorant ridiculous it

All this can only say: You are so lucky boy

We ran into a clever and powerful booksellers touted gotta make you rich and famous

To know whether the novel is written how long how good

Historical fiction evaluation will not be higher than poetry

Literary Status novelists are often not as good as a poet

Do not believe you read more literature history

Outstanding poor poet's fame than wealthy novelist high

People may remember the presence of the poet and the poem

But few people can remember people wrote novels

Do not believe, you can look at our spiritual backbone of China Qu Yuan

People can enjoy with the Dragon Boat Festival to commemorate the novelist is not what it

Our people has only been in place for the anniversary of the outstanding poet Qu Yuan spirit

When our people sincerely for other writers had set up to commemorate the holiday

Ignorance is not at fault

It is self-righteous ignorant people get ridiculed Yanzui

Curse is not necessarily justified

Sometimes shelling attack only shows the attacker know little

Do not think a few books

He made a small fortune on the smug self-conceited

You can deceive and booksellers get together ignorant naive fans

But, you can not deceive and booksellers but knowledgeable readers

A condescending attitude most intolerable conceit

Outrage difficult to commit even that you do not understand Han

You singled out one person you have this whole poetry capability it

There was a poem slightest true poet can you refute Han speechless

Unless you are really lie blindfolded guy

Besides the historical authenticity of the poet's own comment

Ugly works also own conscience says to the reader judge set

Han's worthwhile you dancing and shouting booing evil

Only this insight croak shallow people shout

Yes, you Han wrote, "modern poetry and poets how there"

God let me clumsy poet to answer how are you

The reason why there are modern poetry

Because you write a novel written in a very false

You write a novel writing covered conscience talking in your sleep disorder

Mongolian people also conscience money

Nonsense fictional character

Confuse right and wrong depends on good has

Because you write a novel so fabricated non tease the reader's conscience and intelligence

Reality will have a modern poetry and poetic heart sincere presence

The reason why there are modern poets

But also because this world can not let too many write novels deceive

What is needed is not just false self-fiction dream masturbation

People need is the existence of a sincere heart and poem poetry

Perhaps you may be the world do not really exist Han

The world will be absolutely real poetry and poets

Because: most sublime poetry written in fiction rather than false

Han you stop shelling attack Parnassus really much ado about nothing

Pseudo-poet, poetry is not worth your mix to attack Han

Real poet Han do not you go shelling

These are silly things

Do you have time to go open up your car from the music or fight a good ranking

There is a good book to read it and reflect on their own point

Do not let the bookseller touted exalt you dizzy

In this world we do not know what is too much

The more you read, the more the more you will find that we know know know too little

Do not mix and boring poem argue

Except to hype, otherwise your reputation no good

2009-4-10

The dream talk with my wife

Ying

For the history of poetry is

The poet's own personal agenda for what the pros and cons

To know the development and contribution of poetry

Not by today's Federation of Literary and Writers

Nor is it just to make money by book publishers

Not by fictitious College scholars, professors

Nor is it against the Parnassus poetry mixed trouble, monkeys

Of course, the real development of China's modern poetry

Even under the guise of not by preaching, Tuition, doubts away swindling literary crooks

Indeed, Ying

Development and contribution of poetry

It is unknown intentions folk poetry by the poet

Regardless of whether such intentions poetry folk poet living hopeless misery

But they are the real contemporary poetry, poets

Poems were they alone with their poetic soul of poetry

Perhaps this poem, poets position too low

But their literary value will be much higher than the poetry publisher packing out the so-called poet, writer

Whether or not such folk poets and scholars whether publishers like recognition

Be real poetry, poetic heart of this often only anonymous folk poem by him in

Everything with money, worldly, selfish or authoring package will not come out of the poem by the poet is the highest level

Writing poetry was not the only person phony fake pseudo-poet before

For those folk who really poetry

Affordable social reality nothing of horses and Salon

Publishers just more money blindfolded text traffickers

Please all of us who remember the folk poetry

The only thing we have is our only poetry writing poetry and lonely soul sounding cry in the night sky

2009-4-18

Leave the dream to the reality

I love poems

Poetry may not necessarily love me

In today's the only money in the supremacy of the

Poetry can engage

But can not eat rice

Poetic dreams can not go back to enjoy a dream

However, the reality of life

We make the man but must let the family getting the point

Believe it

Poetry poetry will give people a sad way to go

Poetry will not let good people live happily poetry

Perhaps poetry can really make some poets have love

But poetry decidedly not the poet have a better life

Love Poems may need to decorate a romantic woman to win the hearts and minds

Marriage can be home but need the actual money to support live

Sober now! Poetry faithful

All poor like me "incompetent" people write poetry

Poetry will only be like drunk who put our heart and soul irrigation was drunk

Poetry poetry never let people have what real return

If you thought life like poetry

Then the poem really let you live like a dog useless life

Poetry never really loved any poet, poetry by

Poems have always regardless of the poet, the poem's life and death, success and failure

Simply poem poet poetry sincere heart and pay no demand has to material rewards

Poetry abandon it! All of the poems who

Poetry will only make the poet's life be poor feel lonely

Poetry poet despaired only make today's world can not be real

Poetry and even others will provoke resentment and revenge merciless ridicule abuse

Our society has ever really cherished a talented poet writing

How can our society really respect and support a write only Western painting east poet

Alas! Heaven

We do not need this era poem to life without poetry to cultivate our minds sentiments

Spoof of our time simply to paralyze our heart and soul of our fallen human nature

For the reality of the world is

Their heart and soul belongs only to materialism money

Poets and poetry for them is not worth talking about

Poets

We can not let the cold reality was chilling poem by

We can give up our original dream of poetry

We can not but return to our original real-life roles

please remember! Poetry faithful

We even our own families and live light point

This is not practical than what poetry live with peace of mind, really nice

Our social reality is really nothing more nothing extra to feed a poet

                        2009-5-19

The fishing activities by the city administrators

Gang son of a bitch

Fishing is not a true black car

Not really caught the illegal operators

Black-wolf gang dressed in human skin

Fishing is money

Also caught the real victims

for money

Can illegally "enforcement"

for money

Can Fangshuiyangyu, has helped rejection

for money

Possible collusion, working hand in glove

for money

Dark traps can entrap innocent good-intentioned owners

for money

There are a bunch of your mother born father did not teach the black sheep is favoritism

for money

Bunch of ungrateful son of a bitch is self-dealing

for money

The real road blockers can gang condemned, Peoples abomination

Even if it is a wicked thing will not hesitate to do whatever they want

This is the ill-gotten gains

These son of a bitch is trampling human conscience and morality

This is the shady interests

Black-eyed hanging bunch of wolves are distorting the facts, framed innocent good-hearted people

"Fishing" This shady wet technique is torture of the human conscience door

"Fishing" trampling more than just public power and conscience bottom line

"Fishing" trampled countries also face some of the human nature and moral conscience

"Phishing" is more than discredit the justice and dignity

"Fishing" to discredit the good as well as the present and pure humanity

So bad Invitation to a Funeral "fishing" favoritism "enforcement" scandal

Really amazing, sad disappointment

Heartless unscrupulous as to

Indeed people angry, sad helpless

Such and such "advanced" and "smart" and "fishing" method

It is an eye-opener, really lamented the lawlessness

People ah people

Why sometimes the feet of the brute than tetrapod also serpent

Power comes from the hands of the people and why some people can do whatever they want

And all this done

As head of the department is the most can not forgive sin

All rackets

Not the secret is behind the instigation of its dereliction of duty

Justice lie

Q earth public mind, morality, public rights

Is Nanjing, "Peng Yu case," people did not dare to help the fallen passers

Simpleton gang supercilious look wolf also did not dare to let us do good to help others

Anxious person

The help to help others

Human nature also

Will you guys animals disgraceful feet wolf

You call really difficult callers what to do

Destruction of humanity "fishing" grasping "black car" behavior does not stop

Called among the world helping others benevolent good qualities, how can flourish

Do you really want to do a whole community living in the sackings, all captive

Such and such serpent "fishing" grasping "black car"

You really afraid outrageous? Lightning fire

2009-10-16

Poem is getting bad and people are getting old

Urging them white-haired old

No medicine for bad people

Worldly vicissitudes thing

Cloud heart through sad eyes

Silent, then morals

Empty since the sad old

Although the efforts of the young

God does not wish to frustration with the poet

Empty empty sad sigh

There is a poem in vain belly was no reward

World situation

But dominate the square hole brother! Impressive looking

Money World

Poems such as feces earth! When the dog heart lung

Good day! In vain the people! Not as good as before the Road

Konghenkonglian

A poetic nowhere to vent chamber

Narcissistic

Yong pregnant just because all those little

And who appreciate poetry than on the Road

Empty Beihen

He had close pen poetry financial ruin morals

Gan vulgar husband

Human predecessors only said three meals a mediocre living things

Renyankewei

Good deed goes unpunished

Mediocre little trouble

2009-11-13

The sound from the lawyers

Commissioned by others

Income money not to have to help people ward off evil

Fair words only fair and reasonable facts speak

Defense counsel for the victim and it is not to shirk the law should be punished

Ask the heavens earth

Lawyers conscience is due to the presence or absence of the justice

Lawyer's duty of impartiality can only make legitimate defense in the legal framework

Lawyer

Not for fame and fortune to run around shouting

Lawyer

Although by law the existence and the victim

But, as a lawyer

It must be only for fair and lawful thing to say in terms of the defense

For the wronged to seek justice of judgment

Let's get real justice and effective implementation

Let law enforcement no longer Xunqingwangfa

Let cases no longer be affected by the money and power

Let the real independence of the judiciary further implementation and oversight

Please note that the principal

Speaking of defense lawyers and only under the permission of the law

Lawyers maintenance can only be within the legal rights of the victim

Use any fancy lawyer to evade guilt, escape the law should be punished is wishful thinking thing

Sincere warning to all principals

Lawyers real need to protect the victim is not subject to legal wrongs in vain sentence

Conscience and duty counsel can only be to safeguard the legitimate rights and interests of that part of the client

Just, fair and legitimate is always engaged in legal affairs shall have the character and purpose

Any injustice, false cases as judges and lawyers are the shame and guilt

As police and prosecutors also a shame and sin

Such unfair referees degrading glorious mission of judges and lawyers

Police and prosecutors also degrading the glorious mission

remember

Legal Empowerment of judges and lawyers in the body is intended to be sentenced according to the law, according to the law and the debate

Any confuse right and wrong, black bleached the real world and innocent people is an abomination to the crafty villain

Lawyer

Lawyers not to prove in court that there superior adult eloquence and eloquence

Lawyer

Not only to legal counsel deserved reward but to do nothing

Lawyer

The whole world is just, fair, and legal practitioners involved in

Conscience and duty counsel and never have to stand on the scale midpoint of the law

As a lawyer

Only a just and legal case to fight

As a lawyer

The defense lawyer must do all speech should have a clear conscience, indeed no selfishness asylum lawless

As a lawyer

In public, in science, the law must also be fair and just, and fair and honest thing and Law

As a lawyer

Decidedly not become strong human lackeys, minions, evil accomplice strong endorsement weak oppress innocent people

As a lawyer

It must be on earth right, justice and the struggle does not regret

2009-12-14

Give the good police image back to me

The police

I want to ask

why

The reality of how the police had been with me in mind when reading the police are not the same

I read before reading silly

Or the reality of the police is simply not the case

The police are afraid of a joke

I think when he was studying

Police and justice is the human incarnation of the brave

Our police is to protect people's personal God

Police hearts

Of fairness and integrity, enforce the law impartially

All police really good kind

Able to fulfill their duties, it seems

We can be faithful, serving the people wholeheartedly

I firmly believe that time

The police will Zhifarushan, realistic

The police will certainly faithful to the law, be loyal to the people

At that time, I think

When the police more glorious! More divine! How great

But why

The police

Why such a ruthless reality

My mind already very beautiful image of the police milled pieces

I was too naive ignorance

Police are still really too much negative coverage

The police magic "hide and seek" and other cases

Let me say good police speechless

When

Social realities

I can also do justice

I can also at the beginning of a beautiful image of the police

The reality of the police

Can you answer my sincere

Do you want to wait until the reality I really do not injustice false cases before they agree to turn back

2010-1-4

To the news reporters

As a reporter

Don't misuse your talents

As a reporter

Not more wonderful flower pen

As a reporter you

Only realistically seen and heard reports

For the truth

To the absolute respect and fair maintenance

Made news stories

Also it must be objective, real, credible

Reporters this career

The pursuit of perfection is not the writing on

Reporters this career

The event itself is the pursuit of the whole story and not artificially distort cover

Do not think

Your literary talent

Readers will be able to win plaudits

Do not think more

Your will and insights

We can represent the voice of the reader with the intention

In fact, the true wishes of the reader

Just want to understand the real situation of events

If readers would like to enjoy a wonderful literary talent

The reader is not necessary to select Reporter

They will choose a poet or a writer to enjoy Mimasaka

The reason for the reader to read the article Reporter

All because reporters have written articles indispensable factor News

Therefore, the reporters

Please God you must bear in mind the poet's advice

Do not try to be smart to play your literary talent

Righteous themselves

Reporter where the error is superfluous

As a reporter you

We must firmly grasp the news value lies

The fact that real stories

Tracking restore the original appearance of the real event itself as much as possible

As a reporter you

You do not need to be performance position and inclination

As reported by observation of events

Reporters only to respect the facts and the true records and reports

Other problems

Readers own sense of propriety comment on events in non-evil

remember! Reporters who

Reporters not a painter

Without the need to add a modified pen and color to the event itself

Reporter nor a spokesman for Fangli Yi

Need to gain away misleading views and positions

Reporters uncover the truth can only be the unveiling of a person

In addition

Reporter actions are superfluous

Any whitewash by it

They are contrary to the reporters of their own

Any distortion of the facts or whitewash itself by it

They are not worthy of being a real reporter

Because selfishness away any high praise for others by virtue of

As shameful acts are honest reporter ridiculed the

remember! Reporters who

The real reporters at all times brute force

Reporters also true at any time not to flatter the rich and powerful

The real reporters will respect facts and readers

The real reporters only loyal readers and their vocation reporter

When a reporter to report the facts themselves can not be real time

As a reporter simply can no longer needed

At this time the so-called "reporter" will only become distorted facts fabricator

Such "reporters" will feature only when some stakeholders spokesman

Put white dots

At this time "reporter" just words to please the owner of a text lackeys Bale

Zuoren done such cheap shameless point

What readers face to face their own conscience and their own text

Please reporter who

Do not think your readers are stupid

News filtered though some people may advantageously

Articles can be too whitewash

It allows the reader to taste the ugly face of pseudo-reporter

Man touted trumpeter

What else is worth your readers to trust

Between heaven and earth

Most can not deceive conscience is upright scholar

remember! Reporters who

The pursuit of truth and fact correspondent is

Reporters ask or where it is human justice

Reporter conscience must not deceive their readers

When the reporter's pen and integrity of the heart can not match, when compatible

Our reporters take a pass on the pen and go seek safety in conscience

Or, use the pen endless struggle

With reporters innate conscience reveal the true face of the event

Who is not afraid

Death does not regret

2010-3-1

The last paradise

Shangri-La

Please grant me a pure land

Let me in there to establish a kingdom of pure poetry

In that simple poetry kingdom

I can enjoy the poetry, the free live

In the self-enclosed in the Kingdom of Poetry

I can roam narcissism in the world of poetry

Live a very good life Poetry

In the world of poetry

No noise

No interference

No sorrow

Nor resentment

No benefit to

No benefit to

Some only poetry and human dialogue and communication

There is only harmony and flora and fauna

Like a fairy-tale life freely

On that land clean poetry

I can write poetry all day, grazing, live

In the pure highlands

I could have lived a half farming half read fairy daily life

Pressure did not survive

No material desires

No sense of responsibility for some of the family

There is no interest in money

Some only is poetry yearning for life and indulge

Please people Shangri-La

Poetry gave me a clean paradise

I had this long life in the marketplace vulgar poet to have a peace poem nest

please believe

I'm asking for too much is not paradise

As long as I can hold to be under less Fengyun restless heart of the poem on the line

Poetry nest I'm asking for is not broad

As long as I can hold this poetic world it can

Please be sure to receive my La

Admission to a wandering soul poetry and distressed people

Receiving a return of nowhere poetry dreamer

Students also receive a poetry as poetry live poetry mad man

I just want my world of

Only poetry, no money

I only hope in my heart and soul

Only a dream, not reality

Let all desires into poetry movement

Let all sorrow have become joyful song poem

In the poet's eyes

sometimes

Money is the world's most vicious instigation

It not only directs us rushing toil

It instigated sometimes let our souls evil deceptive

Do something on our conscience not want to do the thing

honestly

In the poet's eyes

Some people and things not as amiable animal

Some people and things not as world wide to accommodate

Some people and things really are not as noble and pure poetry

Please La cherish the original ecological environment

Cherish the original natural ecological treasure that God gave us wonderland Shangri-La

Do not over-exploitation, tourism

Shangri money from outside sources, while

The outside world will give to bring the original Shangri-La ecological damage

Shangri-La will give the outside world really bring the trauma on the holy

Too savvy tourists

Only led astray local plateau already clean heart and soul

Too much money of foreign tourists

Shangri-La will only make people become vulgar and pure snobbery

Please people Shangri-La

Consider a poem's urgent desire

Give him a piece of paradise on earth right

In the poet's eyes

There is the last paradise on earth where

In the eyes of the poet

There is a Wonderland world of poetry

Look - Shangri-La

The sky is so Jamie

Snow is so white

People are so simple

Heart is so pure

Poetry is so intoxicating

2010-3-15

To some advertisors

Do some shameless than the conscience of the world on advertising

When the mouth Products

Why can not realistically mediator says

Lure deceive consumers

This is not so brazen it

You can not put a bad product or equivalent

Also boasts hype like Value

Well Zuoren

Total honesty with diplomacy and conscience.

Do unto others items will not impose on others chaos Recommend

The play two-man show is not so hypocritical deceive Fudge

When you do not face the introduction of goods equivalent

Your self-interest only black heart filled with hypocrisy and copper bromine

I wish all the endorsers

You can sincerely treat their heart and soul and consumers

Do not even the conscience of a few coins are sold out

Zuoren too poor to even the poor should be the conscience and moral integrity

Life really is not advertising this hypocritical Writing

In the same time you hoodwinked consumers

You Fudge it not in your own conscience Zuoren

Product introduction and product boasted that are two different things

When a person's heart straight injustice

Dogs will outlive false advertising spokesperson strong

2010-3-24

Stay away from the small coal miners

Brothers

Please do not burrow for others

In your holes while for others

Perhaps you really are in their own self-dug grave

Perhaps you really are in your family at home missing out

Not just your own tragic fate manufacturing

You bring the family there are endless grief and despair

Close your eyes

Perhaps you do not know

You will only hurt your family

Others show it is only a short sad life of the poor and you lose sympathy

maybe

Your boss coal shed only a few drops of crocodile tears performative

because

Coal bosses have thought more of their wealth is created dream

and so

Even at the expense of your bones also balk

Every accident

Every sad

Mine will not be vested interests

Every sorrow

Every flesh separated

It will only go down a coal mine coal mining brothers

Which accident

What a bitter experience

But also the interests of the coal chain

Bros

Really could not unsafe small coal mines dug holes

His own life will cherish sincere

Their families their loved ones will really care about

In today's money worship prevailed

Others decidedly only deplore their pocketbook

Bros

If you work in an unsafe small mines

If the production can not be guaranteed under the security measures of small coal mines

That bet will only coal bosses riches your violence

That is the only bet their lives and families missing

Bros

Even the hardships of life

Can not only for the wealth of others digging hard work

For their own self-dug grave

Even helpless life

Not only for others but also bloody sweat

For their own little income

Do not believe

Brothers on the eyes are open wide

Which coal bosses are not the wealth of legend built on the bones of the dead miners

Coal which interest groups happy life is not eating and drinking are built among the downhole workers sweatshop

In the coal bosses heartless eyes

Which is not a coal mining brothers will create a wealth of rat holes

Do not be silly

Bros

People are not afraid of any honest labor

People afraid of people stupid brains turn, but turn to

Do then took his own life and family away to create wealth for a small coal mine bosses

Under your adventure

In your sweat, bleed under

Others are only happy families

To complete your life and family

Please brothers must stay away from unsafe small coal mines

To his family no longer make me cry

Please brothers must have safe and secure work only coal mine

2010-4-5

The man is not man, the sea is not sea

Yaokan year

War years

Heshan broken broken country

How many healthy men and women Jie

Shed blood

Defending the homeland on the battlefield

Kill devils, the Japanese slaughter

How many bombs explode justice pirates

How many gun shot aggression Justice

I have vast land invasion were killed or off

I am guilty of the Chinese people die endlessly large

Back to the old dream

Patriotic overseas Chinese Chester

Chen's family tankahkeei

Chuang Southeast Asia alone abroad

Earned under enormously wealthy man

Give all donor countries against Japan

Now the number of corrupt officials, dignitaries, profiteers, actors

Shaving cream to make the country Choi Min

Choi Yang said shift abroad

Banana Life

Unsightly

This is really inhuman

This Yangfeiyangye

This really Overseas Overseas

True patriots who also

This Andean fake, Jonas ocean

All scraping fiscal abandoned ungrateful traitor fake foreign country

All fake foreigners

We do not have the ability to make people shave cream domestic wealth of the people

Real skills to go abroad naked foreigners earn money outside

I and other people do not envy jealous

If no ability to earn money outside of foreigners

Please hang Haier fake foreigners abroad do not come back

So brazen repatriation of people scraping money

This is also spineless person

Abandoned country aspiring Worship

I thought there were false foreign devils

We shall know shame people do not eat too dependent

Also no longer need to return to the domestic money people scrape

Chinese people's money only raised descendants of Patriots

Definitely not support Haier splenetic fake foreigners

On some day in 2010

The money that you cannot understand

See through money

Your mind will be pure

Air thoroughly credits

Your soul will be noble

Many people see through money

Many people also Air impervious credits

Many people will become secular people

Few people see through the money

Air individuals through the credits

Individual who has become a strangely weird people

When your eyes do not have money

When your heart is no credits

Your heart there is no mercenary

Your soul will sublimate in the world

Your noble qualities will live in your own spiritual world

2010-5-17

The song of the drivers

Faithful car

No matter what you are driving a vehicle

Regardless of your driving seat is expensive or cheap

Please when you are driving a vehicle

Be sure to compassion! Life as the most important

Because: life for you and everyone else only once

Because: your car before someone else's loved ones

Similarly, perhaps someone else's car in front of your loved ones have a presence

Please cherish the lives of themselves and others

Please also cherish all the way creatures

Good first, patient first

Caution, safety first

Forbearance and tolerance, give way

Stop for a brighter future

Not angry, not vindictive

Perhaps this is for yourself or for someone else the opportunity to stay happy

please remember

You slow, you let the line

It really is in the sake of your family (or someone else's family) the integrity and well-being

This really is in your Jide your charity

Someone else's poor behavior or wicked drive that is someone else's accomplishment limited

Your tolerance, your patient that you are a noble sentiment driving

please remember

Life, we only have short lives and loved ones accompanied

You drive out of time

Your family is looking forward to your peace and go back to peace

Round and round a happy family life

Really I do not want you to have an accident when driving

Please carefully grasp the direction and speed

The slow time must be slow

The stop time must be stopped

You are in control of the vehicle and not just your life

You drive on the road when it is related to people's safety and well-being

You must bear in mind

Flower of Life definitely can not hurt or destroy in the vehicles we drive

Otherwise, you really are a sinner hateful destruction of life

Your future soul might atone in uneasiness

Your future reincarnation are bound to spend at the wheel with only

Please keep in mind motorists

Truly responsible driving should be like good people like docile sheep rather than like a ferocious Langhu

2010-8-9

The words from Buddha

I Buddha of compassion

I Buddha generous

I ask Buddha to save the poor people of the world

I'm on my heart

Over and over again recite sutras

I have in my mind the Buddha

Over and over again singing the praises Verde

Namo Amitabha forever in my heart

I have in mind the angels of God

I plugged in my heart Buddha cone with a cone incense to worship Buddha

Not good for the heart was led astray to worship false gods

The public is suffering just to clarify my Buddha Ming

Please almighty Buddha Buddha care of your people

Let all the suffering and sorrow no longer come to earth

Let all the evil and greed no early closing

I Buddha of compassion

Let the people have hope nothing Buddha

Let the poor people in the world among all sense of security, medical services

Let the real poor people have food to eat, clothes to wear

Let the world of the poor children have the chance to read and learn something

Offer some work, fair treatment, failing justice, equality

I Buddha righteousness

Let no room between the people of the world have residence

Let too materialistic men and women have changed

Let them not be too excessive desire

Encouragement and kindness

Promote the most glorious work

Not the workers do not enjoy the fruits of labor of workers

Buddha I Come

I am calling you to come in day and night

I am eager to show you all the time gilded

Please grant The Buddha

Qingjiang to Buddha

Please auspicious gift

Please bring blessings

Please bring the Scriptures

Please with wishful

My charity Buddha

My benevolent mercy Buddha

I heart Buddha Buddha Chung Yong Song, Buddhist

I also look forward to in the eyes of Buddha's visit appears

Please breadth of your men and women

Please let sentient beings suffer permanent off wheel

Please let the creatures forever good luck

Please make people happy life in this world of charity

Namo Amitabha

Life helpless

I Xinxiang

Foguangpuzhao

Buddha's heart, such as electricity

Buddha sincere poetry

One poem Buddha

When healthy and happy

When good luck

When equality beings

I quickly made fast Buddha says

Whether that life of living beings must

Buddha's heart always lethal only sustenance, Buddha heart Fragrances

But in reality, yet so helpless, helpless, hopeless

2010-11-18

Give the peaceful world to us

My heart is bleeding

I am indignant at the spewing blood in the Pentium

Every time I see are too polluted rivers, land, atmosphere

My heart will be sad and angry

My heart will be also lamented that her time and time again how small, impotent, helpless

My conscience will once again be stimulated and touched

Environmental pollution was so severe in the back with interest if people can not see what lies

Are they (administrators and managers) in working hand in glove

People ah people

When administrators and managers to become the interests of the chain

Disaster, suffering, contaminated not only the local environment

Disaster, suffering, contaminated as well as the people living downstream

I want to call! I want to shout

I have to say! I thoroughfares

What kind of morals

Human conscience really let Tengu steal yet

Or perhaps some people simply do not exist conscience

When pollution, poisoning, detoxification who only care about their own self-interest when

When an economy of greed at the expense of the public's living environment at the expense of time

When the black-hearted factory owners and some bad officials working hand in glove in time

When vested interests to our health at the expense of creating their Jinshan Silver Sea when

We will call! We must say,

What kind of shit Economic Development

In fact, this is at the expense of the public health benefits in exchange for some of your riches violent behavior

I can not help but grief from the heart

People ah people

People really have to Qianyan drilled yet

The conscience of the people some money so let Uncle invincible distorted out yet

So "developed" economic philosophy is joyful or gloomy

Only money is whether theorists sometimes simply distort the conscience of the culprit

Assessment fair

We need money

We need more living in a clean environment

We need economic development

We need to be more dependent on clean water and air to survive harmless

We do not need pollution - in the way of economic development Duanzaijuesun

We just do not need more human survival in their own way to develop the economy

We need clean energy and energy sustainable economic model

We need to co-exist with other animal and plant diversity of approaches to the development of our human economy

All man-made extinction of species other way to develop the economy of all human beings sin

Most human beings will one day scourge of ignorance stupid behavior

When our life resources are excessive pollution

When we live plants and animals around by excessive destruction

We can no longer allow poison factory owners who do whatever they want

We can not allow more of the environmental protection department in no act dumb

We want to say out loud! We want to shout out loud

Living environment resources are public resources

Public public resources

Living environment resources are not poisonous plant owners resources

Of course, not an individual's personal resources, environmental officials

When our living environment is too polluted

Management is not corrupt and incompetent officials in Xunqingwangfa

Since you regardless of people's life and death away pollution earn heartless dirty money

We may have good reason to poison all the public health benefits of the drug factory to stop polluting

We also have a fair reason to no matter what, environmental officials did not act class

To our future clean living environment

And to our children and grandchildren can live in this world clean

Each of us must be concerned with our own living environment

Please be sure to unite

Jointly oppose all our lives pollution resources

Seal destroy all poison our factory black heart health

When rice flowers and flower frogs can not reproduce

We must scream awakened to some callous heart and soul

We need to use our more practical action to defend our public health

Please God and the poet cries together

We do not just need economic development

We need more clean environment to survival

What we need is genuine and things around harmony

We rather good economic indicators are not too high

We can not let the black heart of the factory owners to deny the pollution of our bodies and spirit beings

The public health benefits are higher than the minority of people will never get rich dream of getting rich

Hearts and minds of the public will never outweigh the economic "elite" who shit theory

2010-12-10

The poet thinking about life

I am glad

My blood flowing poetry

I am also very glad

I live a life in poetry of life

I'm really glad

Every year I have a poem accompanied

Perhaps, I'm not strong in other areas

But what on earth can be more beautiful than life and poetry

For a person who Poetry

Poetry is our poet's life

Poetry is the poet of our flesh

Mission poetry than anything else

Poetry is the poetry of life's paradise

Although most of the real life of impoverished poets

Poetry can be a better world, but shall have the poetry of poetry can give only describe depicted

For the colorful world,

The world is more than just material things of mediocre

The world also needs some crazy person poem poetry to decorate the world where the Poet

For a person who Poetry

Wealth creation may not be their own best poems persons

This world who own many of the pains and for the pursuit of possessions

The poet's responsibility is to create a more beautiful poem in the world of poetry

Let's poetry is so pure show in the materialistic world

People get a higher level of spiritual sublimation

People get the highest level of poetic influence

Instinct Room

Poor people can

But people could not do without their own dreams and struggle

People can also be living down

But personality has to be noble, noble

Dressed can wrap a grudge against beast

Good-hearted people, but do not have gorgeous clothes dress modified

Money can decorate personality punk evil

Poetry can only writing but only to those with a genuine poem

God can give a poem by substance vulnerable

However, God will give his life a sincere poem by poetry, poetry

Because I had the poem to accompany

So, no regrets of my life

I also because the poem is accompanied

So, I still think I sometimes I have a clear conscience

Although speaking as an ordinary human

I had a little evil

Can be accompanied with poetry

My great evil but no

I looks mediocre but buried a real noble poetic heart

Romantic sex is not the fault of poetry

Inconstant but it is the nature of the defect's poetry

These are anyway in a poem by poem and poems before

Our forefathers

This can not be pure, no one is perfect

For poetry are concerned

Why should we care about those romantic poetry section interesting

This is nothing but just add some romantic poem poet Bale

A "good" life, the poet might have nothing as useless

A "bad" poetry who was emotional and happy life harvest

Take my "bad guys" who

My first love, my lover, my wife

Which I did not use a poetic to "swindling" come

When a poem can not use their own poems to win the hearts and minds

This "poem who" is simply a loser poems

This is also a poem before the poet's greatest irony

For a truly smart person is born with poetry

As long as you have before writing poetry

You'll have all you need to think of all dreams

Otherwise, we can only show you the poem was lacking, I did not hang around too beautiful favor

As long as you're not greedy

Poet in spirit and soul will be rich and happy than average

A poem can not have too much money

Poetry can be a person, but must have their own poetry and poetry only dream

If you are a person who has failed anything

Then you do not deserve to make a real poem by

You can only do with a person scribble

The world will deserve your life wretched poverty

remember

Poetry can too vulgar life

Poetic souls of those who can but must live a life of poetry

We can run around like a monk-like in the way of hope

We must have a real poetry of the kingdom in our souls

Perhaps, someone who does not understand the poetry of thought

Then why on earth can understand and appreciate how much

Concert of the

Only fellow poetry chanted by resonance

I and other poems by life really only missing a confidante

2011-1-3

About the Maotai Wine

Small town reputation

Bit remote fame

A drop of Maotai tyrants the world

VIPs general wine

Liquor originator

Awards

Hierochloe Trinidad

Only this one

On the Wine Culture and Historical Origins Mission

Maotai liquor alone dominate overlooking the world

Liquor Need

Who Controls

Maotai is not for high vain

All times

Daqu Maotai liquor famous long

Maotai supreme fear for respect

Maotai wine worthy of respect

He accompanied the hero

Xu asked the general preferences of his life

Maotai in Health

Maotai is also the only King after death

2011-1-25

To the friendship between China and Pakistan

I have a Chinese all-weather friend of Pakistan so delighted

I also China have such a proud Pakistani buddies

History proves

Pakistan chose China as a friend is the most sensible choice

History also proved

China is Pakistan's most trusted and reliable friend

In this world

Only China is Pakistan's only natural ally

Similarly, Pakistan will also be China's most steadfast allies born

Friends

They must respect each other

As brothers

Flesh must co

When a friend

It must be good to each other

When the brothers

It must be a common destiny

Earth

A true friend and brother is the most treasured and cherished

When Pakistan is China's friend and brothers when

China and Pakistan is our brother country

The people of our two countries is that their loved ones

Any damage to the people of our relations is our common enemy

Any damage to the people of our relationship is sin can not forgive the people

Resolutely against anyone to harm the friendship between China and Pakistan things

Please believe the people of Pakistan

Our friendship between China and Pakistan sky high

Our friendship between China and Pakistan is deeper than the sea

Behind Pakistan's always stood the China reliable friend

History and facts prove

China and Pakistan are the most capable of flesh and common fraternal country

Please believe the people of China and Pakistan

Sino-Pakistani friendship will never flower bloom in the hearts of the people of China and Pakistan

China and Pakistan will be the world's most friendly neighbor model

China and Pakistan will be the history of the staunchest and most reliable friend

China and Pakistan is really called adversity

please believe

And China friendly

You will share the prosperity and prosperity to China

And Chinese friends

You will feel China friendly and sincere

China and join hands with the retractor

We will win with music

May Heaven bless

Our two countries will always be good friends! Brothers! Good Neighbors

Also May Heaven bless

We Pakistani friendship for generations! Honest and treat each other! Forever Yours

Let us join hands and Pakistan! And common progress! Create brilliant

Sincerely wish: happy the people of our two countries is long! Well-being and longevity

2011-5-13

The man and the poem

Vulgar vulgar head only hold things

High-quality poetry must use high-quality head taste

Without influence of the arts on the ignorant

People stupid is no need to reward poetry

Just greedily on materialism

Mediocre why the essence

Vulgar rich people just

Poetic Soul without Yong

Notice also

God will make materiality who survived this life only for material

It makes people God has a heart with a poetic world of poetry

remember

Different life

Who needs the same thing

Bliss public phase

Dark dark heart's soul forever

Shameless person will never understand Honor

Hypocrisy lifetime crafty

Poetic kind of translucent human soul forever

Q poetry worthy

Q. The good heart

Ask people original poem

2011-6-16

Waiting for Jiao Yulu coming back

Yulu

You're gone, you're gone

You really gone, really gone

People calling your

People calling your return

come back

Comrade Yu-lu

come back

Jiao Shuji

You can not go

You can not go

You really can not go

You need people

People like you need a good secretary

come back

Jiao Shuji

Your people are ready for you to treat liver cancer

Your people are ready for you to share the pain

You come back

Our good secretary

Good son of the people

You can not go

You can not go

You can not just leave your people

You can not cast aside your people regardless

come back

come back

You people in the hope that you come back

Your masses yearning forward to your return

come back

come back

Good son of the people

You come back

come back

We can not do without your

Our people really can not do without your - Jiao Shuji

So how do you "heart" of the people leaving your

How do you so "cruel" of leaving your masses

You do not go

You do not go

Are you sure you do not go

Jiao Shuji

Your people are ready for you to bear pain

Your pain people willing to block for you to endure

come back

come back

Jiao Shuji

Jiao Shuji

You come back

Your people all the time that you miss the

You people are always looking forward to your return in the heat

Your people are willing to be with you

You and your people happy symbiosis

come back

come back

Jiao Shuji

Knowing good and bad people Cadres

True and false servants of the people know from

come back

come back

Ten thousand people have too many Jiao

One thousand Jiao Shuji still too few people

The real interests of the people of comrades people welcome

People hate hypocritical hypocrisy cadres

come back

come back

Jiao Shuji

People worried about your

People thinking of you back

Sincerely for the interests of the people of the people clearly

Hypocrisy is not serving the people who understand

Who is a good cadre

Who is a good comrade

People all know

People understand

People will really love and eternal bear in mind

China has always been no shortage of self-interest sham officials

China is sorely lacking Jiao style of cadres

Lack most is hundreds of thousands of real Jiao comrades formula

2011-6-20

Respect knowledge and culture

Not to the government to joy

Not as gifted with wealth

All things are clouds

Alone know the hardest seeking to understand

Be naked

Go naked

See how reactive officials to make wise admire the rich man's death look

Real history books

History lesson

All times

Renxinbugu

Baiguan worships money but snob

Human beings

Daru is eternally self-active improvement of the human person

2011-6-27

The man who owe the balance

Ever since the poem

With the presence of the poet

Do not know

In the end is the lack of social poet

Or the lack of the poet in society

Perhaps someone will say

The poet can not write poetry

Society can not lack of presence or absence of a poet

In fact, many people do not know

The poet's contemporary society has been in arrears with the poet's reward

Society has been in arrears with the poet plays a role in rogue accounts

Do not believe, then please take a look at the previous poet

Even poet Li Bai, Du Fu Shi-Sheng

With that they can not only survive writing poetry

Nor with their poetry back and ask for social return

People have been enjoying in unpaid previous poem

In history, the society has been in arrears with the poet deserved reward

Do not believe, ask yourself

We have been enjoying in unpaid previous poem

And we have never paid income returns over the poet's

In fact, the poet of contemporary society should return early poet

In order to avoid unfair things have been in the continuation

2011-7-2

Poetry was contrary

Looking back at the history

How many poets and poetry solitary poor bored

Sigh current economic times

How much wealth buried not only the poet

On the matter of skills

How can emotional poem by undefeated

On the spiritual world

Heaven only knows

Holes poetry and music

Only fellow celebrate poetry by sentiment

A sense of poetry Yi

Hard core materialistic sense

2011. 7. 19

To be a good man

Please do not put as shameless ignorance

With open eyes can not lie

Long with people like you must have a heart

sometimes

One can play the fool

People can sell silly

However, people can not say no conscience lie

sometimes

One can have a thick skin

People can also be loaded to force

However, people can not shameless

Since some people want to be a bitch

There is no need to establish their own brand of what Zhen

remember

Deceived and hoodwinked

Only show their own incompetence and no shame

The reason why people do not say words

It does not equate to endorse or agree with their views and what they do sometimes

Fair, just and fair often only exists in the minds of silence

Sometimes the world can deduce strong evil, no justice

But the people own justice, fairness, justice exists

No person of conscience can be quite evil and unreasonable

Notice of management's good-hearted people will naturally kind and speak righteousness

Please remember

We must make good-hearted person

We absolutely cannot be shameless hypocrisy wicked

2011.7.22.

The life-survival skill of the wealths

Money is not a blessing

It is good enough

How many wealthy Weng

Buried dead Qianyan

With natural cause

Work shall overrate

Do strong industry head

Success understand from the back

Ping funeral

And had Happy Road

Do not block others away

Figure a Lok Weng

Do not let the money slave

Greater risk bits

Homo sapiens is hidden from

2011.7.23.

where is the poem heart

Chi sky high

Poems such as thicker

Unfortunately, today's Poetry

They are unrealistic expectations of the generation

I was born mediocre

Only know how to get the word Poetry and Fu

Box Life

Chinese poetry world

Pen pick moon and stars

Poetry lofty as the sun

Hot heart

Frost universe

Today's world

Money does not recognize people recognize

Even if they have only lofty poetry

Food and shelter can not do nothing

Do anything

A sense of Fu

Why book come out feeling like paper

Poetic asked why worthless

Feeling life

Rensushijian

Only lonely hearts pen this remaining years alone

                                          2011.7.30.

Bad spirit hard to endure

People in poor integrity

Lu Yi broken bones

Capitulation traitor heart

Demons poured urine

Japanese sneer soul trick

Soul salvation is not evil

Exotic difficult reincarnation

Aggression revive ban

Bianshi hell refining

Buddha abandoned Invasion

Hell Hades income

Guicu things souls

Why should the people who

2011.8.6.

Hate Japan, love China

Male audacity

Only Japanese, following the lead of the pirates

Female shameless

After the commitment to robbers, who pride invaders

How many men and women for money Ungrateful

Full sub-string is the lack of money people Ajinomoto

Chinese dignified, great country

Much so weird and things

It is actually the country shame, negative ethnic

Chinese nation has blood in vain

But it is infidelity, lack of filial piety negative States, unjust negative family descendants

Ugh

Lost were forgotten ancestors

Recognize thief parent

It not for the country, nation almost sinners

Where a person I big Chinese nation

Can be responsible for the nose

Where a person I big Chinese nation

Are required to live on ancestral world, live under the nation

Students shall be deemed to have national pride among Chinese

There is also a dead ghost China conscience of justice

2011.8.11.

The degree seller's university

Make wise

You must have an independent personality and thinking

Do stupid

It just does not look a gift horse parrot think

Almost all of the world-class institutions

They tend to have a masterful character

Advocates also the knowledge and wisdom

Almost all the commercial University

Often produced mostly of commercial goods

These University

Not so much a "university" as it is a commercial company

Because: These are for-profit university

Because: These are college students as monetization products

Because: These universities are mercenary operators

So, these are often only produced in the University Act of worships money Baiguan

Where what knowledge shaped shadow master

Put it bluntly point

This is a diploma traffickers ear

2011.9.2.

Begonia poem Dream

How many times back Begonia dreams

How many times tears face

Times and sad

Times and tears

Helpless poet think, more than a dream

All because of a bad break, worried

Rereading Fangweng often "show children"

Leila often sad

But the sad but not Kyushu with

Begonia Akiba into cock

Wang Shi North Central Plain

I also come in Huahai Tang

Mi no more countable

Coin several text Worry

Poetry dream unawakened

Tong flower still beautiful and moving

Helpless Great Han has to go

Ingenious, but Wenzhiwugong

What Li Shimin

Yuantaizu where Genghis Khan

These are historical figures of the old things

But "begonia leaf" people often miss hanging heart

Poor poet inaction

Tong flowers still blooming

Yong Tong pen still

Tang leaves the heart forever

Who round my dream Begonia poetry

So as to avoid the death of shame ancients

What division of North Central Plain

States offering not been forgotten Fangweng

Begonia Akiba shall return

Blood inch inch of rivers and mountains

Yong bone protecting ancient frontier

2011.9.17.

The lives of Ants

Like ants live

Like ants low

Despite the efforts and busy

The situation can be condemned to a life of life never change its pattern of tiny

Ants life no matter how hard work

Ants can not escape his life of hard labor fate

The ants have to accept their fate

Protest and cry his heart only heard

Fortunately, there are ants geometry

Facing injustice ants life

Release the suffering self Complex

Although ants living hardships and lowly

Be humble ant life might be able to have a clear conscience life

The resultant obtained are relying on their efforts in exchange for pay

This is compared with the parasitic life or exploitation

Humble ant life really seem noble, great

They seem so pure, it is peace of mind

2011.9.30.

The efforts of poets are meaningless

Many years

Introduction struggle

Hard to say

Helpless old people sad white empty dream

Zhuolei declared final few drops of poet life miserable

Money is not with people

Flower wait months

Only poetry Confessions

Concert slim

How the world

Where singing

Where poetry Yin

There his talents writing in vain

Half as good as mediocre wages

A sad weeping hills

Angry poem artesian

Good little

Many vulgar Act

Liang poem of epic proportions

Come master

Poetry by the very top life as mud

Acts intelligent poetry

Less than half secular bills

      2011.10.6.

Cheer for many highway toll stations

Dotted toll

As nest of bandits, as everywhere

Extortion of passing vehicles

Each toll station are written on the face of the five characters:

Leave money

Each delegation railing

In fact, a robber in duplicate for money

This is really the way I built

I opened this mountain

I want to live this way

Shall remain money from

Behind the toll "smiley face" of

But it is the coffin shot

Dead face down for money

But I do not know why the world was ashamed

Each charge pawns

They are ill

Robbery of passing vehicles

Every so-called "Highways staff"

In fact, it is the real road blockers

The previous owner is essentially the meat on the chopping block people

Looking at the interval near the toll station

As a good string of pearls

My heart just kept chattering

My feet could not help weak

Helpless sigh

Minsheng difficult

The owner is not easy

Money on shipping

Wool sheep body out final source

2011.10.9.

The heart of the hero

Into a major event

Section area not

There are people within it

On the outer dressed MOK

Not to gains and losses on the success or failure

Not to be imposing pomp

How many heroes

Sword rivers and lakes

Shicai put Kuang

Not on the day

Location unworthy

And lonely

How many things

Q. How God

Man proposes

God disposes

heroic nature

Race against time

On only the spirit of excellence

Mo on the success or failure

He is a hero

The source asked not

2011.10.10.

Shaolin Monks is a merchant

Look left not a monk

Right not like monks Air

See how

How the Air

Shaolin monks are not monks like

True monk

Vegetarian Buddha

Chanting by Gui

Disillusioned

Six clean

Buddha ancestors yearned

Internal organs are empty

Six internal organs clean

Money clouds

Shenma fame

but

The Shaolin Temple is

Not like temple

More like company

Shaolin Temple presided

Not like Abbot

More like the company's CEO

Really money to wear intestine

Buddha weight businessman

Lot of money

What makes the best moves tricks

Should tell the truth

This is not a monk monk

Dabei Temple temple is not

This was not the abbot Abbot

Not the temple by the temple through

Ugh

Wang fat keepers of the temple incense

Scriptures monk bitter

Monks and money Heart

Distorted by the study incense money

2011.10.12.

The poem's authenticity

some people

Mouth claiming to be a poet

The body is not flowing with the poet's blood

some people

Writing on the self-proclaimed himself a poet

The work is a true reflection of a worthless paper full of words

Some wealthy business "poets"

Is the money "hit the" money "poem clothing"

But I do not know gorgeous "poetry clothing" in

Full of belly full of businessmen

Some Beverly's "poets"

Is also busy dealing with the book number traffickers

At their own expense to publish their own packaging "poet" title

But I do not know so waste paper-like so-called "poetry"

Printing was fine and neat

But also in essence is a waste of timber resources

Masturbation, self-mutilation of their spiritual conscience

There are those who can close the official official "poet"

Is also using the special resources for the generous

With the people's blood and sweat support

After satiate

It will write some Ngau Tau wrong words

The object of the class that is required to serve

Such a pseudo-poet, poetry mixed

Such as the Federation of Literary Writers,

this world

Fucking funny

Not a true poet of the people

But occupied the poet's place as "poetry" fill in "word"

The real poet, poet

But rickets with the waist dwelling in their own souls cry

With publishing

Rampant hegemony, dominating the poetry world, poetry

Like rape girls like

The pure poetry, the poet

Yin sound in the "poetry" echoed

The tears of the poem gush like a spring

In the world of poetry

Poetry in the howling

The poem groans

The poem is crying

Poetry in the mercy

The true meaning of poetry

Can only be buried in the folk real poet body

The peak of poetry

Never never succumbed to a pseudo-poem without a poetic writing

Amen

Who in the poetry of injustice

Who is Saving the Poem

Who is torturing the poet

Who in shameless interpretation of hypocrisy

Poetry Ling self-knowledge

Poetry soul self-evident

Today 's poets

Only folk hidden survival

The poem really Yin

Only in the hearts of folk recollection melodious

All the pomp

Will only rape the poet

Pollution of the poem soul

2011.10.14.

The aim of writing and meaning of life

Sometimes

Poetry does not make it out

But feel the poetry useless

Sometimes

Writing is not bad writing

But that the reality of utilitarian society will not allow

Poems to be the United States, no matter how good

Poetry only high-quality soul will appreciate

Article written again fine, deep

The article also has only the cultural mind of the talent will know how to taste

In people only know the time to obtain and demand the material

In the spirit of the poor but there is no shame in the crowd

These creations are superfluous and worthless

The success of education lies not in the teaching of people asking for and asking

The success of education is to let people know what life is

Dedication is the highest value and the realm of life

Poetry creation and the purpose of writing the article is also due to this

Good poetry and good articles will make high-quality soul live in the real life track

Requests and demands often only teach low-quality portrait animals like instinctive material life

Live in an official not for the people, the poem is not for the people, the people only know for their own era

Is a sad era

Is a people without guilt and shame of the era

Is a spiritual poor and rich material wealth of the times

Is a do not speak of virtue and morality, do not speak conscience, do not speak of the era of sorrow

2011.10.20.

On Poets' Ineffective Life

When you ask the poet is the strong life

You are not ignorant in shameless

Since ancient times

How many talented poets devote themselves to poetry in the spirit of devotion

Time like Arrow, poetry heart without regret

How many have a poetic poet of conscience

And which one is the only personal gains and losses without poem alive

When you are laughing at and despising the poet is the low energy of life

When you are teasing and contemptuous of the poet is a poor life worm

In fact, at this time you only know one, I do not know the other

Please open your eyes to see

A poet or poet is no more dazzling than you

Such as real estate businessman Huang Nubo

Another example is the publishing industry in the money by booksellers Shen Haobo and his ilk

I would like to ask

The impure commerciality of the so-called poet

Which one better than you make money? There are economic minds

And who does not live more than you dazzling? There is the so-called sense of accomplishment

Utah is the real estate businessman Mr. Huang Nubo

His wealth may be a lifetime you can not earn it

To be honest

Please do not look in the eyes of Air

Poet, poet's brain IQ may not be worse than ordinary people

But the real poet, poet often love poetic life

The artistic achievement of the poem as their own responsibility

The peak of the poem as a pole of life

Such poets, poets are destined to life as a poem, poetic arrogance

Regardless of the consequences, regardless of gains and losses

To poetry as music, for the poem and live

To poetry as the soul, to poetry for the soul

End of life, do everything

Only for the poetry of art

A certain money and other slaves - vulgar is not ashamed of those who do not

Ru, etc. mortal son, fame and fortune of the Zen how to know the ears know the poem to know the soul

Whirring

The real poet, the poet not to success or failure on the success or failure

Pure poets, poets do not say how much money to pros and cons

The real poet, the poet only to see the length of writing

The real poets, poets only poetic soul on the poetic spirit

All the poets and poets who devote themselves to poetry

You do not have to care about the secular gaze

Philistine pupil will emit a vulgar light

The real contribution to poetry and contribution of the people

Often only Seoul and other people despised and ridiculed

Our folk poets must shout

To the poem Sheng Du Fu proud

Not to the failure of the poet's life ashamed

2011.10.29.

Part III: My poems and my life

God is calling for the real poet

The horn of poetry has already sounded

The poet of the charge must be courageous

A hail of bullets fell on the front of the Warriors

The back of the shot in the fall is a shame

Fight it

Poets

Impure poets must be rejected by the essence of poetry

The real poet must take up the important task of poetry

The pursuit of pleasure of the false poet will only put on "poetry clothing" to cheat

The real poet with poetry will emerge in the folk

Although the pseudo-poets are now also in control of the discourse of the right to speak

But how can they hypocritical poetry can not summon the true meaning of poetry

No matter how pseudo-culture who plays a poet, poet

But the real outstanding poets, poets will only come from the people

The emperor can not be shameful staged the emperor's new clothes

Slipping whips can also be insincere

But the real interpretation of poetry will only come from the real poet heart and soul

The rich pseudo-poets published more poems

Hire more trumpeter

It will only be silent paper

No poem of the poetry of the recitation will be shouting loudly again

Can only bring out the surface of the art of flashy atmosphere

The real poetry will only come from the real poet heart and soul

Gao Jie's poem soul must be detached from the vulgar public places

Where the holy poem to accommodate the slightest false impure

2011.11.3.

Why the first class poet cannot life happily

No matter how precious the glorious verse

And no matter how beautiful the United States and the United States poetry is unique

Can since ancient times

All of the material society

Are based on material

The nature of greed for virtue

To the material skills for the glory

To have a wealth of wealth for success

How many nonsense is not social

To the door of the Air

To the dog eye treasure

Diamonds abandoned roadside

To respect the food stool

Whirring

This is the lack of wisdom and civilized society

This is a materialized society

This is material rich and spirit of the poor and weak society

Ugh

People foolish

Not illiterate, not I do not know the book, not unreasonable

People foolish

Is to know the book but do not understand Thanksgiving figure

People foolish

Is to the wisdom, wisdom, injustice and disrespectful self-righteous

People foolish

Is to absorb the essence of the poet but do not know how to return the poet's reward

The poet lifelong essence of white take, white, white reward

Sad to the extreme

Poets like the spirit of the priests for the human essence of refining the spirit

People prefer to support the nonsense-like novel author

Because: people figure is masturbation, since the music, from the stupid, since get

The novel's false and deceived as the real plot and sink in

After all, people and society have not evolved into poetry society

The holiness of a poem can only be perceived by a poetical person

What a first-class poet had to live like a beggar-like live in the world

The poetic heart of the noble but also not the reality of society

The versatility and value of poetry is geometric

Do not believe to see this from ancient times

First-class poets and a few people are not poorer and poorer

2011.11.8.

The achievement of the bad people

Vulgar people to luxury cars and cars as a sign of success

Bumpkin and nouveau riche will spend lots of money to build its glorious coat

Outside the strong majority of the stomach did not expect

Not much cultural knowledge of people will use the appearance to make up its meaning

Brand-name clothes may be wrapped in a school of ignorance

More beautiful dress can not conceal their superficial knowledge

Do not believe, to see those so-called successful artists

These actors are master of Huyou

Chestless ink but can also and self-interest of the director working hand in glove

Low-performing clown, but also often occupy the public resources to play with the public

Private activities is the so-called network strength

Ghost grinding behind the number of money demons and monsters

Bad media may be playing with the audience and ignorant of the conscience and wisdom

Do not understand the shameless actors who also consider themselves very successful

I do not know what the world brain damage? Conscience, art value of geometry

Even if it is undone pants rules also want to play a fame

2011.11.9.

Poet lives worse than pig

I am a poet

I am not a businessman who will make money

You asked me when my wife can go out to make money

I do not know

I do not know

I can not answer

I can not answer

Although I have a poem through the poetry

Although I have a poem across time and space

But now if you sell for money

Someone has to buy

Someone has to buy

I am a waste

I am a waste

I want to shred my poems

I want to delete my text

I want to stir my poems

Can not be recycled waste home

Can not be recycled waste home

I have to go out

I have to go out

I have to send my poems to the streets

I have to put myself on the street

I have to sell poems

I have to make money

Say what is false

Say what is false

The hardships of life make the poets who float high on the earth become vulgarly low

Need to live the poetic heart become selfish shameless

I have to make money

I have to live

I am also a person

I also want to eat and drink Lazard

I have to put grass on my head

I have to split my poems

I have to share my poems

Pass off the Keguan

As long as you are happy

as long as you like it

Take it is

Take it is

Cheap to sell

Cheap to sell

How many will do

How many will do

Selling light pull down

Selling light pull down

Not very

Not very

People can also be sold

People can also be sold

Nourish not

Nourish not

This person lazy

This person lazy

Only to understand the poem lyrics

Only to understand the poem lyrics

Life is incompetent

Life is incompetent

Stupid one

Stupid one

Feed the wolf is acceptable

Feeding the wolf is acceptable

Would rather pig

Would rather pig

Do not raise this person

Do not raise this person

          2011.11.11

Don't marry a poet

Wanting the stars is not a way

Down-to-earth have a way out

Fantasy empty fantasy

At home is no good

Real

Oil and salt

Selling poems can be non-human

The poet is the same as Huyou

Star no poetic

Ang Wang will only empty

That poem at home without profit

On the meaning of only intestines stomach empty stomach

Making money is the best policy

Talk about poetry will only harm people

Support the family is the primary

Warn the world

The poet is useless

Life is incompetent

Fantasy is more than reality

Mind wide through the earth

Heart than days high

People live with poetry

Foot on the clouds

Poetic horse

Not down to earth

Do not eat fireworks

Rhetoric

Huyou life

Love can be

On Marrying

Marriage without happiness

Home poverty such as washing

Life without

Young and old suffer

Do not marry poetry

Stomach hungry palpitation

                2011.11.12.

An interesting poet

You give me a bite

I will give you a world of poetry

You give me a dollar

I will give you a poem you can not forget

In a materialized society

There is such a rare clown

A life of low energy clown

An unintentional clown

A cloak to ignore the housework

A poem will only fill the poem

A mysterious treasure of human life

A clown who does not know the world

In the world of poetry

There is such a poem crazy

A poem for the students of poetry

A poem for the poem and live

One will only use poetry to foolish wife poem crazy

One will only use the dream to intoxicate his wife's poem crazy

A wife will only keep the poem crazy

A wife to eat soft rice poetry poetry

On a: not on the high society of poetry

One: the unbearable and the bad guys of the people of fish poetry

A: There is no survival skills of poetry crazy

With his wife's words is summarized as follows:

I am a useless clown

A phase does not phase, to look not appearance clown

A clown that is neither seen nor used

A martial arts is not effective, the second child of corruption and incompetence clown

A bed of waste, living waste of clown

A talk cheat, mouthful of clown

A coaxing his wife will only love the heart every day clown

A life in the helpless super-clown

A naive, silly plus ignorant clown

A starved to death have a copy of the poem

2011.11.13.

Everything is meaningless

When some people shouted to how to attach importance to the development of poetry

You will put these words as nonsense

To see the real life of the poet

You will find life in the bottom of society poet how lonely and helpless

When hungry people talk about what the great cultural development

You do not think this ridiculous and sad

Hungry people want to talk about how to solve the first hungry problem

Not many cultural people say what the great cultural development is simply nonsense

An intellectual can not get the attention of the community, how can there be any culture at all

A supremacy of power is only a society of power

A society that does not abide by the Constitution and the law is a society that is not qualified to talk about the rule of law

A society that does not treat people's livelihood will not be a good society

A society to let the monopoly group to crush the interests of the people's livelihood will not be the society people expect

We hope that society will become better and better

We also hope that the culture can get good development

We look forward to the poetry will be some spectacle

We also hope that the poet can a decent life

We also hope that the real contribution of intellectuals can get the best treatment

We do not want to see people in the eyes of some officials as ants-like slightly

We do not want to see some officials do everything they want

We hope that the people can really enjoy the sincere service of the civil servants

We do not want to flicker

We do not want to deceive

We hope that our people's livelihood will be the greatest degree of care and improvement

We hope that our society is truly people-oriented, with kindness and conscience to others

What we hope is that we all contribute to the country and society and not just to know

We do not want officials higher than Hongru! Powerful invincible

We do not want hay bales better than wisdom! Money is on the hero

We do not want more power to trample on the Constitution and the law

What we hope is that everyone is equal before the law

What we hope is that everyone knows the law, the law and the law

What we hope is that all law enforcement officials are unselfish, fair and honest

We hope that men, women and children are amiable and friendly

What we hope is that our society is a harmonious human society

What we hope is that our society is a high quality people society

honestly

We really hope that the talented poet can have food to eat, to wear clothes, to create peace of mind

We also hope that our society is a perfect society

We hope that our society is an idealistic society

We really want our society to be a poetic society

2011.11.14.

Life with wife and poem

A sleep sleep naturally wake up

Poetic poetry

No poetic time by the way

Life is always leisurely leisurely living

Do not work

Do not make money

Do not want personnel

Do not figure money

Do not wear a mask

Not empty with people

A wife possessor is really good

Free to live

To spend

And poetry for pleasure

With the poetry of God

in reality

Wife and sleep with his wife and love

Poetry in the magic

Possession of Poem and Dissemination of Poetry

How peer poet

There is a wife and a poem of the day how

Realistic enjoyment

Poetry in the magic tour

A wife's day is better

A poem of life is sweet

2011. 11. 24.

Guilin's beautiful landscape

There are not mountain full moon

Water does not look at flowers

This mountain must be Guilin mountain

This water shall be the Lijiang River water

Hill, where not

Water, where no

Shan on Shan

Guilin how to win the roost

On Water

Li River only count the Qing River water

Nature, between heaven and earth

Miao on the wonderful in the mountains and water

Absolutely never in the landscape god together

How many places beauty resort

Which is better than the Guilin landscape of the wonderful color

People in the middle of the painting

Can not tell the mountain, that water, the man, that painting

People in the bamboo stand

With the landscape into the United States into the camera

Hill has more show

Water is more beautiful

Hill has a few odd

Water there are a few wonderful

Guilin's mountain show, show on the show in the water

Guilin water the United States, the United States on the United States in the shadow of water

Landscape of Miaozai, Miao wonderful in the days of God made a mountain floating

Really name the world! Unparalleled in the world

Guilin is the United States and the United States landscape is absolutely unique

The world water stunning stunning, absolutely holy and quiet water

People to Guilin

Evil is also good

People travel Li River

Internal organs fresh and clean, no evil heart and evil heart

People to Yangshuo country

Human nature perfect, do now human nature

Lamented Guilin

Worthy of "Guilin landscape Jia Tianxia" the beauty of the title

Beneficial to physical and mental health of the health

Should choose Guilin, Yangshuo, Lijiang River

Want to cultivate the heart to raise awareness of fish fun

Xingping fishing village is preferred

2011.11.30.

Dream of Guilin

Health when the dreamer

Death to chase dream ghost

More than half of life

Forty buried half buried

Not enlightenment

Dream of Guilin

For the poem crazy

For the poem live

How much money energy for poetry and die

Make a fool

not realistic

Landscape soul

Dream of Lijiang

Do not consider the amount of money Jin two

So far, no matter how many cent fall

Discredited see wife and children

Porridge eat vegetarian snail claw Hill North Lane

I hope in the future

"Guilin landscapes together Tiancheng" Bo to the old wife smile

To retort curse nagging

Guilin living room to eat vegetarian Buddha

White as a monk back

2011.12.3.

My wife is so good

Not at home

Go out to understand cheap

Guest house thinking wife cut

Warm blanket

Love language

Affection thick too small

You, I, I, Love

Enthusiastic care

Is very affectionate happiness

Fish and water fun Xiang Huan

Night embracing sleep

Now celibacy

Life is lonely

Cold and warm no one to intervene

Hungry I do not know

Empty empty wife without partners

Is very lonely miserable suffer

2011.12.4.

Good and bad to be a worker

No matter how pretty you dress up the city

You are still just insignificant migrant workers

No matter how tall buildings you build

You are a group of people look down on the migrant workers

Even if you how to contribute to the city

Even if you can let thousands of families have a warm home

People will still despise you for the country to the people

Although the development of cities can not be separated from the participation of migrant workers

High-rise buildings occupied by the land although it is inseparable from the cheap slightly wins

Regardless of migrant workers and farmers how to make sacrifices for the city

The city still will not appreciate

No one will appreciate your migrant workers

No one will sympathize with the lost land of farmers

The city is such a ruthless

Reality is so helpless

City people do not want to live

You migrant workers have to do

City people do not want to eat the bitter

You migrant workers have to eat

City people do not want to suffer the pain

You migrant workers have to suffer

Low work needs your migrant workers dry

Great urban construction also requires active participation of your migrant workers

When the city needs your migrant workers

You migrant workers must come

When the city does not need your migrant workers

You migrant workers must go

Build a good city is the responsibility of your migrant workers

Clean up the city is also the responsibility of your migrant workers

For migrant workers do not have complaints

City of the building you dry

Every city in every brick or have your migrant blood and sweat

Every family in every one will not be grateful, thank you migrant workers hard to pay

Home - is not really your migrant workers can give

Some of the landlords in the city is indeed dig a lot of money to buy

Only eat the most bitter is your migrant workers

The most tired is your migrant workers

Take at least you migrant workers

The loss is the most landless farmers

Do migrant workers do not complain

The city needs you to do the work of migrant workers

The city does not require you to do the work of migrant workers to go

Do not nostalgia

Do not pity the city life

City life It is not your migrant workers can lead a life

The enjoyment of the city that you are not some of the enjoyment of migrant workers

The migrant workers are only the passers-by for urban construction

Come when you come

The time to go when you go

The construction of a beautiful city is not related to your migrant workers

Dress up again gorgeous city is only the city people's homes

Roll back to your countryside

Return to your country

The farmland in the countryside needs you to farm

The rations of each Chinese person may be settled by your peasants

As farmers will have to be compromised

As migrant workers will have to accept fate

Identify your own life is to agree with your history

Sacrifice the time of sacrifice

The abandoned when discarded

Do not compare with people

Do not fight with others

Do not talk bitter

Do not call tired

You may be born this life

Come hard to come

Hard to go

Call every day should not be

Called land to work

Good self licking ask wound

In the city when you need to come

In the city do not need your time to go3

2011.12.16.

Good to talk about virtue

Heart to do good

Human bile edge of Health

Micro-bit yet to forget this

People poor still know good

How much power

Only some people dressed

There is little to do good deeds

Bad Germany often pregnant

Fake kernel of the mouth often open

Parasite

I do not know what Thanksgiving

The rich people

Do not know the power of conscience equivalent

People to the points

Heart to good

Light without losing the meaning of life

Rich and wicked still shameful

More money to die in vain

Lack of knowledge and some people empty bone

Animal nature is still more

Lack of human wisdom

2011.12.22.

Poor people and the new year

Afraid of the New Year

Afraid of the New Year

Home wash and New Year

Last year was good this year

This year also made wins old year

Years sad

Years sad

Year after year sad

How to pay out money

Where does the human condition come from?

Friends and relatives need to entertain

Bit by bit for the money to pay

Money is difficult for filial earners

Poor ghost hard to be generous

Hospitality is not good pro-sparse

Bag deflated as a courteous person

There are old

Under the young

Poor house is really difficult

Do the old workers no one wants

No art weak boss too

Business is not the material

Born not the boss phase

Forty early

Sixty back

Both dare not say that old and tender

Even the embarrassing era

Sit on the sidelines

News strange year after year

How many characters Jide good

Erjin face

A pound of meat

Twelve food cooking love

People face

Tree to skin

To act in good will

But I do not know

Perform their duties

A clear conscience

Is a good big Dade good officer

2011.12.30.

What does my wife look like?

Wife is a stranger to acquaintance

From acquaintance to love

From love to get married woman

Wife is a blood on your unrelated woman

However, the blood on your unrelated woman is better than blood relatives

Because: wife is a woman can have children with you

Because: wife is a bed with you a total of pillow woman

Because: wife is a woman can live with you for life

Because: wife is a can spend a hundred years with you, always love to spend the woman

Because: wife is a total fate with you, with the breathing of the woman

Because: wife is a closely related with you, love woman

Because: wife is a woman can not replace the other woman

In this world

Only the wife of such a woman can be fully integrated into your body

In this world

And only his wife will have a lifelong love you with a woman

In this world

Only the wife will be most concerned about, the most caring, most care about your woman

Unless, your woman is not a woman with your heart and soul

Otherwise, there is no reason his wife is not your most intimate, most love, the most relevant woman

In this world

Only his wife will be a life can be entrusted with a woman

Please take good care of his wife, love his wife, cherish his wife

The fault of the past and his wife's bad good over

Re-make a good man, good husband

For a real love and really care about his wife's good man

Anywhere, anytime

But also rich and poor

We have to make a true love of his wife a good man, good husband

2012.1.9

The good Wuliangye

A glass of wine Wuliangye

People happy every spirit of cool

With the toast

Jun Mo worry

Festive cups crisp ring

Fortunately with the table

There are people

Auspicious wishful acquaintance

Happy things

Friendship long

To drink

Cup Mo stop

Affinity together 1000 cups less

Discourse speculation happy

Both drink

If Wu Liang

Sweet and delicious taste of the throat

A five-day liquid poetry to poetry

Shixian Li Bai fairy wine

Poem Saint Du Fu Li Baiqing

Ancient poetry famous take alcohol

Aroma long mellow taste

Ancient Porcelain Square

Secret unique

Years of elaborate aging

Just right full wine

And the king drink a total of Chuan Sheng wine

Evergreen with the hero

2012.5.22

I would like to live in the world of poem

I admit I'm not the strongest person in life

I also admit that I am the low energy of life

Please do not say anything to me the survival of the fittest, discomfort were eliminated

These Darwinian theories of evolution have long since disappeared from my mind

I admit

My body is in the material world

I also admit

My body still exists in the world

However, I have to admit

I was born in a poem

I live in poetry

My heart has drifted away from the flesh

My soul is early poetry

Although poetry in the eyes of the world is not worth mentioning

Can really good poetry will only survive in our "man of God" in the

Please do not make fun of me

Not material skills

Please also do not make fun of me

Not the economic beach-goers

For the material to grab

I admit I am weak

For the possession of money

I admit that I am poor children

Because: My heart is not material

Because: my soul is not economic

My heart is in my poem

My soul is only in my poem

In a world of poetry

Here to talk about money that money

In the kingdom of a poem

Here only on poetry

Between beauty and ugliness

Here only poetry to experience and judge people's face

Please do not tell me that life's trivial things

Also please do not say to me on earth boredom

For a pure poet

Really too boring

The world of poets belongs only to poetry

Every pure poet will be willing to live in the poem

If he is a true poet

If he is a real poet

He will live in the poem

He really can only live in his poetic world

Not allow the outside world to bother sinking pure poetic heart

2012.6.9.

Safe milk

I can believe the cow

But, I can not believe the milk

I know: cows eat into the grass

I also know: milk cow is squeezed out

However, the bad on bad people

Greedy heart often can not stand the temptation of interest

Contrary to the conscience of the really happen

Pure and impure, shoot the chest ask yourself

Security or not, ask yourself

Too many cases confirmed

The safety of milk is always entangled

In the world

Why not as good as the legs of four legs honest

Trust is always being played by profiteers

Conscience is often trampled on by money

Please the world's mother careful attention

Buy milk at risk, purchase must be cautious

In order to baby 's health

Please mothers try to use their own breast-feeding children

Mother's breast milk is the best milk

Mother's breast milk is the most pure milk

Mother's breast milk is the safest milk

Mother's breast milk is the most affectionate

Relatives of the dairy milk than the conscience of people reliable

2012.6.15.

Save my last good will

No matter how decadent life is

I will retain my last little poet dignity

And no matter how much I live to be driven to distraction

I will retain my last poet nature

Born in a materialistic world

My poetic heart is very disturbed

Live in the money arena

The spiritual poet will be the subject of a massacre on a conscience

I stare at the poet's eyes and watch the material world of money

I feel my heart and soul survive in swords

I put up my ears and listened to what was happening

I listen to is a Han Shasheng mixed with the howling tragic

I have been on the battlefield of material desires

However, I was defeated

My weak heart and soul, but universal money overlord

I wore clothes

I also covered a

I put on a helmet and a mask

However, I finally defeated

I can not beat others

I can not defeat materialism

I can not overcome the material heart and soul

Because: I am a poet

Because: I am a poet of inspiration

My heart is not protected

My soul has no armor

My naked poetic heart how to fight, but fierce material desires

In this materialized world

I admit I lost

I lost a worthless

In this materialistic arena

I admit that I am not a real material fighter

In the kingdom of poetry that I have

Materialized warriors will not care and cherish

Although, I have tried to instinct alive

However, I really can not

In the eyes of the real poet no spiritual life is the most horrible life

In the eyes of the real poet life without poetry is the most intolerable life

The real poet sees poetry as life

The true poet sees art as a soul

Poets really feel that poetry is more important than matter

Talent is more precious than gold

Inspiration is really luck

When you give me the low energy of life

Please allow me to retain a poet's final conscience

When you despise me as a wretch of life

Please allow me to keep a pure heart of a poet

Perhaps, I do not deserve to live in this intrigues of the world

Perhaps, I really do not deserve to be born in this material hero of the times

However, I live with poetry in this powerful spiritual world

Because: I have a real poet heart and soul

Because: I have the last poet nature

Even if I failed in this material world

I will be a spiritual winner

A poem to the world of poetry alone poem madness

Do not believe, to open your eyes to see my poems

In the poetry of artistic accomplishments, I am not as good as Jun

But you are living in the material

And I live in poetry

2012.6.21.

Poet's debts and dreams

Bank of text messages like Suoming spell

Between the lines in the urging of repayment

Property company calls ringing non-stop

Every phone is chasing the property fee

Pay, no money

Do not pay, to water and power

Only the sun and the air better to say

Sunshine, not money

Air, not money

There are poets engaged in the work of the soul not to money

Poetry and art are not money

Leaving only the poet's flesh and blood there is little use value

Cook to cook even though the knife

When the creditors can naturally disappear

When the annoying claims debt no

When do not understand the business poet can feel at ease writing

Can have food to eat

Can not be driven to earn money to support his wife

The poet's dream is just uninterrupted poetry

OK? Amen

2012.6.24.

Poet's soul and body

I use the poet's unique eyes fired the wisdom of the wizard

These spiritual spirits are the poets who devote themselves to poetry

Outstanding poem soul Ordinary heart can not understand

Because: they use a mediocre attitude towards poets

This also can not understand the inner soul of these poets

And I, because read too understand the more I feel sad and fear

My sadness is not whether there will be a poet to repeat the same mistakes to death poems

I am sad is the materialistic heart will quietly kill the poet's heart and soul

I am sad is that people's hearts will continue to materialistic and utilitarian

All this is to erase the hope of the poet

And these places will continue to kill our innocent poet

Where the fragile poetic heart can withstand such a materialistic torture

When utilitarian heart is an end

remember

Cold than the knife and gun is also terrible

Numbness of the heart and soul is also poison than poison

More poetic poetic heart can not affect the longing desire

Spiritual soul may be the end of life to interpret the call of poetic heart

What poetic heart? Material boundless

The world is proud of its wealth

Unique poet is ashamed to miss poetic heart

In the era of materialized domination of the world have a conscience poet had to cry alone

Any Tianjiao poet if you want to survive in the world

Your poetic heart must have special protection

These protections must be able to withstand the indifference of the eyes and insensitive heart and soul

If the poet really want to survive in the world

The poet must practice the skill of the avatar

Let the poet's soul live in the world of poetry

Let the poet's flesh to the instinct of animals to survive

Only with these superb ability to protect the poet's survival

Both the poet and the poet are in the poetic heart and the body are trying to cultivate the person

2012.6.25.

The lonely poem heart

Read the loneliness of your heart will be strong

Reading the loneliness of your soul will shine

The poet must be lonely

The poetic soul with the inevitable inevitable

Poetry is not for work

Poetry is only for their own spiritual insights

Joy and sadness are in the process of writing have feelings

Writing poetry really is not for what

Writing poetry only to his own feelings in the form of poetry recorded

Although the young have wanted to succeed fame, to succeed

However, it is the ignorance of youth and self-interest caused by vanity

Now the happiness sentiment is lonely

Is the feelings of the lonely poetic heart when writing poetry

Is a lonely poem in the poem to write poetry with the same happy with the poem

Happiness is really one poem, poetry and people in the same fun

Poetry and heart fusion, regardless of each other

When the poetic heart and material desire to make when

When poetry and philistine brother fraternizing

At this point the poetic heart has been vulgar unbearable, not worth mentioning

When the poem soul really is not from the real poet body

This poem soul must be vulgar and snobbish

Mediocre heart and vulgar soul is sad for the poet

Philistine mentality, how can we make a good poem

In the eyes of true poetry: poetry is not really compatible with the philistine

Poetry does not make vulgar people

The poem will not make false poets with the wind

Poetry will only make a real understanding of poetry, poetry, a nice ring

Poetry will only in their own spiritual realm of the soul of the statement

Believe it

Poetic heart is always lonely

The poet's soul never solo

Eager to walk with the public it is not poetry heart

Lonely poetic heart will always live in the poet who alone

Excellent poem soul is always lonely

The great poet must be alone

Do not ask him

Only poetry heart forever

Even lonely

I have poetic heart forever

My heart alone

My soul is alone

                2012.6.28.

Heros drive carefully

In the district where you drive the car is very fierce

I would like to ask:

Whether you're showing off your car or showing off your driving skills

You are in the car or in the manufacture of fear

When you step on the gas pedal readily

You really think you're imposing

You really think you're glorious

When you are proud of the ocean

Do you know someone else's life is in your dangerous driving

You also know that other people's happiness may be destroyed under your wheels

You really do not know what is dangerous driving

You really do not know what is ignorance and brain damage

Your brutal driving will only harm others

You are ignorant of the only left to their own regret

Please drive all the friends know how friendly and patient

Quality of the driver will naturally open the car was smooth

Not the quality of the people in the accommodation area to drive the car quickly

Do not take life for granted

you only live once

The family is like a fragile porcelain dish

Do not bring fear and danger to passers-by when driving

2012.7.1.

Poem is better than writer

The poet is the real player of the mind

The writer is downright plagiarism

Regardless of the poet and writer to admit it or not

Poets have been wandering in their own minds

Writers have been in their own novels set up

Perhaps, this argument does not recognize the literary world

Perhaps this kind of spiritual play can not give the poet bring material benefits

The poet first thought is the spirit of feeling

It is impossible for a poet to use a writer as a writer for his work

The poet can not for their own interests in the poetic heart of false

The poet would rather have sentiment in his own soul

The poet will not be willing to have the fraud in the poem soul

The poet can be scandalous

The poet will not be submissive in the soul

Poets can not live without poetry

Poets can not exist without the soul

The poet may have no money in his pocket

The poet is in the inner world is full of hot poems

Poets can look like a beggar to despise

The soul of the poet is the spirit of the monument is looking up

Do you believe

The poet is the true spiritual Taoist

The poet is the real player in the mind

Poet in the poem chasing a poetic dream

The poet has always been a prophet in inspiration

The poet does not become a writer

Because the poet does not want to be an outright story liar

Poetry is also not in the novel and the company

Because the pursuit of poetry is sincere rather than false plot masturbation

Poetry is the spiritual saint

The novel is a lie trick

The poet is a frequent visitor to the inner soul

Writers are vulgar people in the hearts of sellers

Poet is playing the heart of poetry

The writer plays a fictitious plot

Poet by poetic heart and cause resonance

Writers rely on deception in exchange for recognition

The poet is the real player of the mind

3. The writer is an outright plaintiff in the novel

Poetry can be heard in the lobby and read aloud

The novel is openly deceived

2012.7.5.

A poet does not follow the rule

Families do not need poets

Families only need husbands to make money

Families do not need poems

The family only needs to be able to solve the economic needs of life

Being an incompetent husband is unworthy of having a marriage

As a man can not earn money really deserve to have a family

Admit it

Pure poet will only love to bring love when the passion

Pure poet will not bring his wife to the happiness of marriage

Pure poet will only bring sweet to his wife before marriage

Pure poets do not bring happiness to the family

A husband who does not make money is not a good husband

A man who lives only in poetry is not a good man

Do not blame the world ruthless

Only blame the poet innocent

Do not complain about poetry returns meager

Only blame themselves are not really Superman

Can not practice to the realm of human world

Life is materially based

Families to make money as the primary

Poet Du Fu deserves to starve to death

Dante, Pushkin to China must not survive by poetry

Poetry reward really reasonable

Poet treatment is really high

Who can survive by poetry

Superman is not a fool

2012 7 7

Poet should be punished

As a poet

You're poor

You are guilty

You do not have the ability to make money

You are guilty

You focus on poetry

You are guilty

You are a pure poet

You are guilty

You live a poetic life without income

You are guilty

As long as you are poor and connected with the poem

You are guilty

In a materialized society

The poor are not qualified to write poetry

In the eyes of utilitarian people

Poetry is useless

Poetry without money

Do not believe, look at the eyes of those philistine

Which is not utilitarian

Which is not materialistic

I do not insist that all people love poetry, poetry

I also do not insist that all people should live a poetic life

Why the world can see the pure poet so hateful

The poet lived a purely poetic life so unforgivable

The poet is really guilty

Why the world can not accommodate a large poetic heart

The survival of the people must be material to life and death

please forgive me

All materialized people

Please let me live my poetry

In the world of poetry

The poet really has poetic self-sufficiency

In the world of the soul

Only the spirit of the poet's soul is not material

Perhaps, the poet simple

Perhaps the poet naive

In order to poetic heart fly, in order to dream come true

I recognized it

I admit that everything by the material people have the final say

I acknowledge that the materialistic society dominates the world

I just want my poetry can continue to live in my heart

I just want my soul to be with my poem

I know I hate

I also know that I am guilty

I know that I do not work in the grain

I also know that I just want to write poetry lyrics

I am guilty of a heinous crime

I let the material people feel bad mood

I let the Almighty materialist sometimes embarrassed

I am shameless, I cheeky

I have nothing to gain, I parasitic guilt

I know that poetry is not good

I know the poem is slim

Why do not I wake up

Why do not I repent

I'm the substance

I am the material desires

I am the utilitarian

I want to live

I want to survive

I want to survive

I want to support the family

I want to make ends meet

I want my family to see hope

I'm the substance

I am the material desires

Poem damn

The poet is guilty

Vulgar active

Poetry without material benefits

Poems dead matter

Whirring

Social support can not be talented poets

Life without Psalms

Du Fu's death and lack of pity

Why do poor dead only understand poetry ear

Why is hopeless and poetic heart does not change

The poet is guilty

Poetic heart can be punished

My heart off

2012 7 10

The hundreds of mertis of poet

Alive, it must be vulgar

Alive, has no dignity

Alive, how many people like dogs to eat

Alive, how many people flocked sheep

Alive, how many people self-esteem can not protect themselves

What the dignity

What self-love

In the world of rolling things

How many people still able to protect themselves

How many conscience this security

For themselves and their families

How much heart has changed

How many men distorted heart

Come out

Who would dare to rhetoric

Who would claim to be the conscience of the whole red

In the material world

Clean heart a few

Temple above

How many people talk

Lobby

Who is not a gentleman

People are not ancient

But poetry heart eternal

Poet song

Poet poets are solitary and proud

I pen, my heart eternal

My poem, my soul from high

Whirring

This life never Panlongfufeng

Swear to death never write a word to the powerful

Silent cold on the sentient beings

I can be responsible

My poems are good

     2012 7 13

Worker on the production line

You need not think

You do not need to think

You only have to repeat the production action

You only have to keep up with the pace of the machine

Your hand is not your own hand

Your hands are just manipulators on the production line

You are not an independent individual you

You are a part of the assembly line

You just have to keep up with the pace of the production line

Accurate, timed to do the part you have to do

Repeat, repeat, repeat the production action

2012 7 18

Feeling of lottery lover

I have been using my hard-earned money in the intermittent support of the lottery dream

Why bizarre winning is always not my copies

Why lucky stars are always so far away

Why do not so many awards come in my head

Why so many awards are always so amazing

I would like to ask the lottery center

I can not vote or other people's ancestral graves in the smoke

I learned the number of surgery probability is not proficient or shake the prize machine does have a mystery

I am not good enough or my bad luck

I was too utilitarian or my luck to arrive

I worshiped the Buddha

I asked to sign

I do not kill

I have a vegetarian

I cherish the Buddha's heart and admire the Buddha and the Goddess of Mercy

Why can my merit is done in vain

Is my selfishness is too heavy or my heart does not change

What others can be bizarre in the award and I have nothing

What can others benefit from the welfare of the cause and I are making contributions

Buddha is laughing

Guanyin silent

My love is like the sun

My Jide is boundless

My heart is charitable

I Buddha boundless

2012 7 20

Guilty in front of the poets

Do not you see the tears of tears

Do not you see the ancient soul sigh ghost shaking his head

Looking into the year

The Tang and Song Dynasties

Chinese poetry world word heaven

Heavenly poem deter the world

Which foreign barbarians do not bow

Many pit father nowadays

The total victory in the Western towards me

Do you not know: Longju Oriental for the Holy Land

Disciple Yang Yi Qi Sheng Tianchao

Cold look at today's poetry

Talented poets

Turn iron into steel

Yangmao not off, evolution defective

How can the side wins the right way

Poetic blindness ignorance

Poor clown

Do not care for the progenitor Yang Yi boast

Spoiled ancestors

Long others ambition, destroy their power and prestige

Ancient soul poet complained to thick

So incompetent

Long weep is not as good as the ancient poetry

2012 7 21

The feeling of doctors' parents

Learning medicine is not to make a fortune

Learning medicine is not to make a living

The purpose of medical science is to lift the public's disease

Make money is not the purpose of medical students

Rescue is the duty of doctors

All people involved in medicine should understand

It is the humiliation of the doctor to obtain the maximum benefit from the patient

The benefits of any medical services must be enough to stop

Any rely on medicine and profiteering behavior is contrary to medical, medical ethics behavior

Want to make money should not be engaged in medical work

Want to medicine only as their own living skills is best to give up a doctor

Because: your income is from the patient body

The doctor's profiteering means a very unfair treatment of patients

The doctor's income in the medical profession is given can not be profiteering

Historians have followed the practice of medicine can not just for the money

The duties of the medical practitioner embrace the humanitarian spirit

Medical practitioners themselves in the Jide virtues

Talented doctors save the people among the patients

Miaoshouhuichun line in patients with the disease

Medical person heart

Medical parents parents heart

to be frank

Hospital Ye Hao

Doctors worth mentioning

The fundamental purpose of practicing medicine is to save lives

The hospital as a for-profit company to operate that is evil

The use of medicine as a tool to extort money that is in the Kengren

So and so, only the soul of those who would be so despicable

And only the soul of dirty doctors will be implemented as that

Although, the hospital needs to operate and develop

Doctors and nurses also need to live and support their families

Everything can be a clear conscience

Everything should be righteousness first

When the doctor can not be covered with copper odor

When the doctor can not cure the soul ugly

The benefits of medical services are not the ultimate goal of the physician

To solve the patient's disease is the highest purpose of hospitals and doctors

Any act that is practiced solely for the sake of money is unacceptable

Any act of using a hospital as a for-profit institution is an unforgivable act

Please all the doctors understand

Although the doctor is not God

However, as a doctor must practice with the heart of God

Kindness is the foundation of a doctor

Kindness is the soul of a doctor

Practicing medicine really can not be just for money

The ultimate goal of practicing medicine is not for themselves and hospitals

The ultimate goal of practicing medicine is to fight for the public disease

The remuneration of a physician is only a by-product of the course of practice

The highest state of the doctor is for the disease and medical, ecstasy

This high realm in reality is indeed slim, difficult for doctors

Can be used as a doctor who must do their best to pursue

Doctors must be bound by the highest medical ethics themselves

Doctors have to treat people with noble sentiments

Because you are a doctor

Because you are the patient's life savior

As the doctor's heart and soul must be broad in the public

As the doctor's mission glory

Please all medical doctors for the music

Ask all the doctors to save the surgery

Talented physician big grace in the world

2012 7 25

The life reflection of poet

See through the troubled world

Your heart will be sad

Read the world

You will feel helpless

Believe it

Society is a huge arena

All kinds of characters are in their own way in the fight

But some people have won the defeat

Some people laugh and some cry

It was also desolate some ecstasy

Winner may not husband

Lost may not be a hero

Sentiment of the above said

You will not just live in the material level of people

Read the works I have done

Your soul will be OBE

Believe it

The highest realm of life is not in matter but in spirit

The most despicable living is not in the appearance of life but in the inner soul

2012 8 10

Good bye, Chinese score team

Do not look at Chinese football can live longer

Read the Chinese football may be folded life

As you believe it or not, I believe anyway

Forget it

This life in order not to torture yourself

I decided not to watch Chinese football in the future

I fight but you, my eyes can choose to escape

Your feet are foul, but my heart is not hard

You play your game

I can play but you

You play still have money to close

You can play the same stinky dazzling

You can still play the game bad media

And I'm different

I saw, maybe I have to pay the tickets

I saw, maybe I have to stay upside down black and white

You lose, I can only live my own gas

You do not live up to expectations of life is the Tell me

You can play this kind of football for generations

You can also play more smelly feet like this

and I

I really can not afford

I really can not see

My spirit has limits

My money is meager

My life is not that far away

I can not accompany you

I look down

I can not play

Chinese football

You win

China's internationals

You man

You can afford to lose

You play for your fans

I can not afford to lose

I can not play

I can not accompany you

I can only choose to escape

I can not accompany you to win

I can only choose to lose

I planted, the Chinese football team

I just ask you do not say anything to me the victory or defeat is commonplace

Nonsense friendship first, race second

These are for me to pull the eggs

These are for me, I do not know shame to say

You can be long-term to be proud of

My self-esteem and ambition can not afford such a long time to torture

forget it

My head is white

Decades of Chinese football dream made me miserable

Long frustration makes me no interest

I have to get rid of this hobby

Fans of this false title no problem

China's football team

You make me dream no longer

Chinese football player

You play with yours

I will break with you

I can not see my eyes

With its long-term hopeless look better than breaking up

And his lifetime watching this wimp of the game than the exile of self-state of mind

2012 8 13

We must save the skillful poets

In the material world

Poet's weakness is not the fault of the poet

A true poet may have more fantasy than reality

Spirit is better than matter

Poetic nature of the pure poet

Materialistic vacuum

The poetic elf can not compete with the layman

Poem of the noble but poem interpretation

Believe it

Materialistic injury to the poet soul is too cruel

Money of the heart and soul to the poetry of the heart appears to be extravagant

It is difficult for a pure poet to have an advantage in the place of material competition

Believe it

In a country where poetry once prevailed

Not a great poet will only make people blame

Believe it

A great poet can not get out of poetry only Hongru shame

Believe it

Outstanding poets will be inspired beyond the sentient beings

Believe it

Utilitarian heart and soul will only survive in the vulgar mind

Please open benevolent atrium

Do not let the poet's heart feel cold

Do not let the poet's grief out of the final roar

Secular world or a pair of real eye

Vanity of all beings only vulgar

Days in the call

In the call

Please save our truly talented poets

In the era of materialistic

In the world of money domination

In the human world intertwined

Please save our talented poets

So that the world's most pure poet can survive

So that the world's most talented poets continue to create

Please let our kind heart fill with love

Please also let us red hot chest and issued a human warmth

Please believe

The real poet is also more valuable than the panda

Please also recognized

The genius of the real poet can not be met

Believe it

The poet of independent personality is the supreme glory

The real poet owner stands civil

Believe it

Very poet of the world poems

The poet is full of talents

Action it

God looking at the secular people

Action it

Eye of the owner will only be far-sighted love

Please use our practical action to influence the cold poetic heart

Please also let our true kindness companions

Because: our poets in creating a brilliant

Because: Our poet in casting a monument

We have no reason to give up the real poet

We have no excuse to shirk the love of the talented poet

When a poet only focuses on our spiritual creation

The people of the material industry have the responsibility to give the poem should be made up

2013 7 27

Life is so real

Materialized human nature is ugly

The artistic heart and soul will appear perfect

Over the years

I have been struggling between the two

The former, too realistic

The latter, too spiritual

I have been looking for a compromise in the balance

But no matter how I find and adjust

I have done out of the vulgarization of the private interests of the soul

I'm trying to hide my ugliness

I also try to beautify my material desires

I can in any case cover up and landscaping

I can not hide my hypocrisy and material desires in real life

I thought about a better life

I also imagine poetry as perfect

However, I can not

In reality there is no such a beautiful life

I have to find in reality and poetry suitable for my living law

I also had to separate reality from poetry

I finally understand

To live must be realistic and vulgar

To be poetic and material heart to be separated

I finally understand

Too vulgar heart without poetry

Too poetic soul will be divorced from reality

In this dilemma

The poet had to be physically and mentally separated

Want to live to live must be vulgar and realistic

Want to think of the United States to pure material soul must be completely buried

The poet is like the spirit of the spirit to explore the human soul world

Poets, like gods, do not need material to survive

When the world is deprived of poets material poor

Ignorance and ugliness will be confirmed in reality

How many poets of the tragic end of the declaration of material desires of people how cruel

Spiritual wealth has always been paid to share free of charge

Shameless desire heart invincible

The spirit of the robber without thinking Thanksgiving

Desperation can only poetry masturbation

And the poem is alive and happy

With the vulgar nausea

Who is pure and noble

But poems shouting

Who can I care

Poetry soul dare

Worthy of life on Earth

2013 8 21

Life is floating and poem is forever

We have good reason to share the poet's spiritual wealth

We also have a free pass sentiment sentiment poet's inner soul

If we feel the spirit is barren

If we really need poetry to cultivate

We will of course share the spirit of the poet all

The Poet's Inner Soul

The poet's spiritual world is not forbidden

Material soul of soul from shame

Lack of mind only know to obtain

Materialistic heart will not respect the spiritual soul of the poet

Whirring

Please do not blame the money of the mind

"Ruthless" how will appear in the minds of people who are fine

The heart and soul of worshiping money is not moral

There is no shame in the mercenary soul

Willing to lose the poet heart of poetry

The spirit of the poem soul Tieshu bloom

The unfairness of the poet can be seen

The tears of grief are always self-contained

Sadness and pain can not save the poet's sad fate

Good poetry can not withstand the inherent indifference of the secular

The spiritual soul of the poet is always shared by the public good

The deplorable death of the poet can only show how the secular heart of hypocrisy

Creating the spiritual wealth is the sacred duty of the poet

The soul of the world can not miss the poet's spiritual psalm

The color of life can not cover the poet's flashing soul

Bai Na and white robbed the poet is also helpless

The spirit of generosity of the poet how can get the same generation of recognition

The grace of poetry and a few are grateful heart

Charity money can win charity reputation

Dedication can only exchange for poetry eternal chilling

Why does the poet's misfortune continue?

Why the heart of the world never guilty

Perhaps

Ignoring the poet's existence can highlight the spirit of man's hard work

perhaps

Poetic soul of the precious only the poet will understand

Believe it! Poets

Low-run pen can raise a fairy and saints

High-quality nature of the soul is inseparable from the excellent works of moisture

The Poems of Laurel in Literature

Recognize it! Poets

The presence of poetry does not affect the daily life of others

The absence of the great poet is the national and national tragedy

The heart of mediocrity can be poetic

Noble soul who can not influence the poetry

Understand it! Poets

The soul of the mentor need not be too care about

The poet's mind is wide across the earth

Forgive the secular bar! Poets

Not all minds can escape the original evolutionary bondage

Not all souls can escape selfish nature

Understand it! poet

Brave sacrifice yourself! Poet

Light the spirit of the public soul to be ecstasy

Climbing poems of Mount Qomolangma will die

Go ahead! Poetic heart fearless

On the way to poetry, there are only warriors of faith

The soul of the temple itself detached heart and soul

Believe it! Poets

Spirit of the gas station only public welfare

The great poet is the spirit of the soul

Do not consider gains and losses

The poet is the great spiritual saint

The poet is an outstanding soul mentor

The poet speaks of spiritual devotion

The poet asked for the inspired prophet

Believe it! Poets

The true poet is fearless

The poet of the poem

Poetry will be eternal

People will be suspended

Stomach can not have

Abdominal empty stomach

2013 9 11

Soul back to the poem way

All suffer the suffering of the people of secular life

If you like

May wish to follow the poet on the spiritual baptism

Purification of the soul has reached an urgent moment

The dust of the soul can no longer support the hypocrisy of the heart and soul

Give up the secular life of intrigues

Follow the poet Zen to realize the high quality of the soul

Believe it

Greed of the vulgar heart never-ending

Desire unlimited self-interest heart and soul will make you a lifetime of mental fatigue

Give up the excess demand

Purify unclean heart and soul

Lost the psychological comparisons

Balanced utilitarian mind

The perfect soul comes from the self - improvement of mind

Abandon the boredom of the earth

Poetry with pleasure in the poetic space

The highest state of life is not how much property

The highest realm of life lies in the spiritual cultivation of the highest soul

The heart of charity is not how much to eat vegetarian how many Buddha

The heart of charity lies in the inner merciful

Please understand the world of the heart and soul

Life is too short

Many temptations

Mortal mediocrity

Snobbish shameful

A well-deserved

All the secular glitz will return the dust

All the charity heart has cycle

All the evil heart and soul is bound to hell

Human nature of the poor earth shaping

The abomination of the soul itself is created

Please listen to the poet's poem soul

Do not let your life live in desires

Do not let yourself die to the soul dirty dirty shameful

Believe it

Living in the marketplace of materialistic heart and soul

The purity of the mind is self-discipline

The soul of the stalwart from the personality

People can moderation inaction

The soul can not die to no clean

Life can be lonely wandering in the world

Personality can not be attached to the trend of humiliation self-esteem

I believe the poem soul eternal

I believe that material desires without peace

With poetry and live self-purification

With the soul and character from high self

The Spiritual Charm of Faith and Poetry

Envy the purity of the poet heart and soul

Spirit lies not in appearance

The soul does not lie in the clothes

For the noble spirit alive superior

For selfish material desires to survive a mean life

2013 10 12

The dragon from the poor house

Twenty-five contained poetry life

Ten million times to crack the text recast

So far only the whole village Miaojing a family

Night bed looking roof

Significant month shift stars turn

Cat and mouse chase

Xingyue perforation

The stars are bright

Or is now or dark

Moon full moon missing

Or implicit or implicit

Wind and rain insight into the life of the house

Sun and rain

No money to take care of

Fear of fear

Watch the sun and the moon has two years

Pass to the gas

Even heaven

Dialogue Jade Emperor as unimpeded

Buried for many years

To write poetry

Concert is slim

Lengnuanzizhi

Bole death

Maxima surviving

Hateful domestic publishers actually no pair of eye

Talent as cattle feces

Money eye view Junjie

APC American Academic Press

Only is the move

Do not ask a hero source

Xiongcai masterpiece see the world

Dragon storm days

Promising future

Look at the world of poetry

Won the literary crown

I come to the world poetry

Bifeng by surprise to be absolutely brilliant

Knowing the grace

American Academic Publishers

2013 12 3

The poem to save the average life

Struggling with an enterprising spirit

Materialism is only selfish

People can pay for the life and work hard

People can not be greedy for life without regrets

God can create a common human nature only for selfish and alive

God can not determine the real soul of the poet

To see through the wisdom of God should have

Understanding the selfishness of human nature

God will be sad and sad

Believe it

Many people can not escape being enslaved by money for life

Many people live only for the sake of life and despicable

Live only know that material desires

Living only know greed and infinite demand

Money worship, profit-driven, Chong Quan's life is everywhere

Sadness is not just bad human nature

There are people who are insatiable

Contentment and a few people really understand and understand

Live for their own conscience and a few people really can do

How noble and distant is the place where men and non-begging are sought

See through the Red

Monks and nuns will be a monk and seek Buddhist comfort

Heart with the Dharma

Can not bear to see the Red dust battle

I believe that God can not stop people's greed

I believe that the soul of poetry will seek the inner purity and tranquility

Poems can make human nature good

Soul goods can make the character from high

Poetry can cultivate vulgar heart and soul

The soul of the poem can freeze the nature of human nature

Please secular crowd stopped profit-driven pace

Seriously look at their inner soul

In this materialistic world

How many secular heart and soul must be baptized on poetry

And poetry

Heart soul translucent

Conscience self - protection

Poetic nature of the good will save people greed and bad

Earthly and only poetic heart can still save the selfish folk soul

2014 2 10

The poet selling poems on the street

I saw the devil devouring the soul

I saw people kneeling down toward the money

I saw the eyes of God despised

I saw the guanyin shame was speechless

I saw the naive poet selling poems in the street

I also saw the poet thought that his broken poem is the gods

Will be able to save all the materialistic people

Will be able to save people no longer on the money and the right to worship

But I do not know in the materialistic world

The poet is as ridiculous as a mantis

Under the knowing is not for the next

The poet is duty-bound against the trend and on

The poet had to embark on the spiritual altar

In the materialistic carnival but the poem heart alone wake up

The poet had to for the ignorant people to restore the self-esteem and conscience

The poet wants to use his sincere poems to influence the soul of material desires

Poets want to use their hot poetic heart to change the indifference of human nature

Poet really with a pure poetic heart in action

Poets hope to save more vulgar heart and soul

Poets hope to save more snobbishness

Poets can know where

Material heart of the soul of the holy soul as early as waste

The prophet of the poet as Dasha

In the world of money as a measure of success

The psyche of the poet is as devastated as a bronze

The poet himself became a clown of life

In the cold street

Poets are still selling poetry

People are still laughing

The poet hungrily sends out his inner call

To the streets of the soul but forgotten

The poet is too kind

People are too materialistic

The spirit of the poet can not save all the soul

Materialistic heart and soul with a poet of the lovely laugh

Poetry in the sale

People are laughing

Soul in the air

The soul of the competition continues

When the poet's expedition can also

    2014 3 13

The true poet living in their own heart

Vulgar eyes do not respect the poet

Walking the body without the spiritual soul of the poet

In the ignorant crowd

The poet is a weird alternative

Recognize it

Poets can not bring substantial benefits

In stressing the real benefits

The poet is just useless

Do not complain about the coldness of the poet

In a society where reality can no longer be realized

The poet really deserves to be despised

Because: poetry can not eat

Because: poetry can not wear clothes

Too pure literature does not have much market

The essence of the poetry of this no real usefulness

Life may not be the existence of poetry

Life may not be the poet's shadow

Really

Poets will only cranky

The poet will only romantic

The poet will only point in the spirit of the soul country

The poet can not sweat for the country and the nation

The poet can not bring you real good

The poet is really useless

How can the poet be the glory of the country?

Poet how can it be the pride of the nation

The poet is only a shameful parasitic

The poet is only the material consumption of people

There is no need for the poet to care and care

Lazy poets deserve to suffer

The creation of spiritual civilization of the poet is not worthy of sympathy

How starving the poet should be

Ignore the existence of the poet

Ignorant and ignorant

Poetry public service is not worthy of recognition

The essence of the poet can enjoy wantonly

Building a rich material society can be invincible

Glamorous appearance can be glorious coat

Believe it

Brain residual will be ignorant

Ignorance can only be shameless

Vulgar meet the low

Snobbish regardless of old and young

Believe it

Poetry heart can sense the world

Poetry heart can weep ghosts

Poetry heart but can not affect thousands of years of ignorance

Poetry heart can not affect thousands of years of numbness

Self-extinguished it

Pure poets

Adhere to poetry creation is no way out

Boiling the text only boil the words of the family

Spiritual poets can only live in fantasy

Harsh environment immortal also difficult to survive

Adhere to the ideal will only burst

The future of the poet does not spring

In the vulgar era without poetry

Poetic power is only a product of joking

The glory of poetry is only to use the face of the ancients to paste

Shameless third-rate poet represents the level of Chinese poetry

Poetry mixed and learn to speak with the false legend

forget it

All the pure poets

We are just living on the edge of the alternative monster

Let the shameless pseudo-poet on behalf of us

The stage of poetry is only for them

The right to speak of poetry is also grasped in the hands of others

What do they want?

The yearbook of poetry is made up of them

The arrangement of the poets with their preferences

They want to how to forget

Chinese poetry is only pseudo-poet's clothes

Chinese poetry is only a pseudo-poet's plaything

Let them continue to work hand in glove

They want to tout whoever touts

Dogs hanging sheep's head is always so smell incense

Mutual interests of everyone understand

A pure poet has no connections

There is no platform for poets' poems

Spirit of the wizard do not know what

Excellent poetry collection published without money

The poet's soul is wandering everywhere

Poet's sad can not tell

Whirring

Fools are often held high

Junjie often buried

Realistic interpretation of shameless hymn

2014 3 22

The city is a mill machine

The city is a huge cement mill

High-rise buildings are grinding teeth

The streets are grinding

The crowd is milling

Grinding every moment in the rotation

Mill in the grinding teeth and grinding between the flow

Mill grinding, regardless of day and night, will not stop

The human struggle can be sustained and can last forever

Some people are weary wear

Some people have no conscience

Some people are worn to death

Some people have been worn as animals

however

People still willing to act as a mill was grinding, grinding

Milling of life or music in the mill

Pain and music

No one can escape the grinding melody

The city is more beautiful homes

Grinding is a relentless purgatory

2014 3 28

The meaning of a poet's life

An old bones

Living a few decades of life is still a sense of their own small

Cold concept of the situation

Life is short, unpredictable

Thanksgiving God

A small home self-inductance happiness

Poetic heart fortunate three students

A cup of tea

To poetry as music

A bottle of liquor

Not the mouse generation respect the hero

Chest million rolls

Ignoring the world material desires

Whirring

Life is sincere

Life never bully

Kindness is still fundamental

This life does not bear Zhongliang

Be kind to conscience

Do not treat people with fraud

Feel good

Personality, dignity can not be without

Sentiment in this life

The joy of life lies in amusement

The true meaning of life comes from introspection

Literati poet to make life

Emotional intelligence to repair the heart first

Villain villain to greed as the nature

Want to do what they want, ruthless

Sue fu

There are a few poetic heart of the world

The world is a bad day

Who can keep the old saying

In vain to read poetry without money

2015 3 31

The happy parents in the Heaven

My mother has been away from us for eight years

Father also drove the crane to the west today

He pursued the love life with his mother

No longer willing to separate with her mother

Believe it

Paradise will be happy

Not old

No disease

No time

No parting

Everything is as it pleases

No bitterness

No tears

There is no poverty

No bullying

Everything is so equal and sincere

Everything is so warm and harmonious

Believe it

The gods in heaven are passionate about their parents

The days in paradise will be fine

because

It is less than the jurisdiction of the Red

because

It was once upon a time of equality of life

Believe it

Refined Faerie will be more beautiful

Earthly troubles can no longer carry the aspirations of parents Sheng Xian

B: No, children

Some things have gone beyond your ability

Not everything can be achieved

B: No, children

Doctors and nurses sometimes do nothing

Respect time

Respect for reincarnation

do not be sad

do not Cry

Parents do not love their children

Mom and Dad just to a distant place to live

Believe it

Father and mother in heaven will be happy

Mom and Dad's love will continue with the eternal

Heaven is beautiful

Soul is very light and very light

The reincarnation of life better than the earth

Do not miss my mom and dad

Mom and Dad have a life of parents

2015 6 9

Get ready for the war, friends

We can not control the Japanese policy

We must be prepared to prepare for the war

When Japan's new security law allows overseas military intervention

Tokyo has been in the war to restart the valve

Islanders to go is their aggression of the older generation of the road

Believe it

Japan's geographical environment determines the inevitable expansion of Japan

Yamato's people have always been not many good people

Throughout Japan's History of Foreign

There is no one that does not do harm to its neighbors

Who would believe what the "Sino-Japanese friendship"

Who is self-deception

Who say what "a strip of water"

Who is ignorant and stupid

I would like to ask

Have you ever seen robbers do good?

I would like to ask

You have seen militarism to save all beings

Also ask

Japan is an aggressive country

Japan as a victim of many wars

It really does not pay for every aggression

Did it really repent of the suffering brought about by the war?

Do not be naive

People to settle in order to be prepared

If you do not see the island countries in strengthening their armaments

If you can not see the island in the opening of the war of the valve

You really is sad

You really are ignorant

Forget the pain

History will repeat itself

Give up preparation

The state and the nation will suffer irreparable damage

Believe it

There is no benevolence beneath the bayonet

Guns only smoke

Japanese militarism is by no means friendly

Fantasy pirates lay down the knife, the site became impossible

Islander's character

The table hypocrisy

Vicious heart

Do little good

Many evil

Bully soft

Death does not repent

Insidious cunning

Shameless loyalty

Wolf of the points

Non-good generation

Sober it

Compatriots in the country

We do not want war

But we can not kill anyone

We yearn for peace

But war can not be our own

We fly the dove of peace

But someone wants to shoot a gun

We can not have the evil heart

But we can not prevent the human heart

My fellow citizens

As civilians

We also have to contribute to the country for the family sweat

We must always keep a clear head

For their future generations to prepare for war

From now on

We must do what we can do to prepare for war

Less to buy Japanese goods

It is equivalent to less after the Japanese bullets to shoot us

Less travel to Japan

Equivalent to less after the Japanese artillery bombardment of our own

My fellow citizens

Really have to do something for the nation for the nation

Really have to do something for their own descendants preparedness

Before things do not forget, funeral division

Do not let "nine one eight" repeat

History will not believe in tears

History will only believe reality

Do not let yourself pay for bullets to shoot yourself

Do not contribute to the Japanese economy again

Enhance Japan's national strength will increase our future damage

Weakening Japan's national strength will weaken Japan's future anti-us

Prepare it

People

Maybe a day of war will come

Comfort will only ruin the country and the nation

Always keep a watchful eye

Peace and prosperity will only anesthesia with our own heart and soul

We will only push us into the abyss

Boycott of Japanese goods

From now on

Boycott of Japanese goods

From each of us Chinese people start

Boycott of Japanese goods

For their children and grandchildren do war preparedness

Boycott of Japanese goods

Let the war come no more

                       2015 10 14

www.ingramcontent.com/pod-product-compliance
Lightning Source LLC
Chambersburg PA
CBHW050423240426
43661CB00055B/2253